# CONSERVATION ISSUES IN LOCAL PLANS

# CONSERVATION ISSUES IN LOCAL PLANS

First published 1996 by English Heritage
23 Savile Row, London W1X 1AB

A catalogue record for this book is available from the British Library

ISBN 1 85074 625 7

Edited by E McAdam
Designed by Nick Cannan

# Contents

**Chapter 7 Development for housing, commerce, and industry**



**Chapter 8 Development in the countryside**



**Chapter 9 Infrastructure requirements**



**Chapter 10 Minerals and waste disposal**



**Chapter 11 Tourism and active recreation or sport**



**Acknowledgements**

English Heritage, English Nature, and the Countryside Commission wish to thank Land Use Consultants for their assistance in preparing the advisory notes. The research and advice was drafted by Carys Swanwick and Lyndis Cole of LUC, guided by a Steering Group comprising Graham Fairclough and Mike Coupe from English Heritage, Graham Culley from English Nature, and David Brooke, Judith Feline, and Roger Ward from the Commission.

# Foreword

This is the second volume of integrated planning guidance to be produced jointly by England's three statutory conservation agencies, English Heritage, English Nature, and the Countryside Commission. It complements *Conservation issues in strategic plans*, published in 1993, which focused on the strategic planning process at regional and county level.

The present publication is aimed at local plans prepared by district planning authorities, and is also relevant to the preparation of Part II of unitary development plans and mineral and waste plans. It offers planning authorities practical advice, including checklists and example policies, on how to incorporate an integrated approach to conservation and the key principles of sustainable development into the plan-making process at local level.

We expect this guidance to be relevant to all district and unitary planning authorities, irrespective of the stage they have reached in the plan-making cycle. Forward planning is a continuous process, for which much information and analysis are needed to underpin policies and to ensure that they represent informed and sustainable choices.

As with our earlier joint guidance on strategic plans, we do not pretend that this represents the last word on a complex subject. The debate about sustainable development and how to put it into practice will continue, and our views will evolve accordingly. We will monitor the effectiveness and continuing relevance of this guidance and revise it as necessary in the future.

For the present, however, it represents the three agencies' considered advice on the treatment of conservation issues within the local planning process. We commend it to your attention.

CHRIS GREEN
Chief Executive English Heritage

DR DEREK LANGSLOW
Chief Executive English Nature

MICHAEL DOWER
Director General Countryside Commission

# CONSERVATION ISSUES IN LOCAL PLANS

# PART I GENERAL PRINCIPLES

## Chapter 1 Introduction

### Background

1.1 This advice on local plans is produced jointly by the Countryside Commission, English Heritage, and English Nature and concentrates on our common interests:

- the landscape conservation and public access interests of the Countryside Commission
- the archaeological, historic building, historic area, and historic landscape conservation interests of English Heritage
- the nature conservation, wildlife, and earth science interests of English Nature

When we refer in the text to 'our interests', we mean all of these.

1.2 The new advice replaces and expands on *Countryside and nature conservation issues in district local plans*, published by the Countryside Commission and the Nature Conservancy Council in 1990 (CCP 317). It draws on the experience gained from drafting earlier documents, but we have also consulted widely, including making written contact with all the District Planning Officers in England, and have taken account of the comments received. We also held a seminar to discuss an early draft of our conclusions. We reviewed a sample of the new generation of district-wide local plans to provide an insight into the way that our interests are being dealt with and to provide examples of policies to illustrate good practice.

### The need for new advice

1.3 Since 1990 a great deal has changed in the way in which the planning system operates. The original study, *Countryside and conservation issues in district local plans* (CCP 317), introduced the idea of an environmentally led approach to land use planning to help to achieve sustainable development. Since then, and in line with the Government's biodiversity and sustainable development action plans, the concept of sustainable development has been placed at the heart of strategic planning in the UK by Planning Policy Guidance note 12 (PPG 12). It is also reflected in the policy stance set out in PPG 6 on town centre and retail developments, PPG 13 on transport, and PPG 15 on the historic environment. Guidance on conservation issues must reflect this changing agenda.

1.4 There have been important changes in legislation, especially the Planning and Compensation Act 1991, which makes it mandatory for all local planning authorities to produce district-wide local plans. National Park authorities must also produce plans for their areas. The 1991 Act establishes the primacy of the development plan, so that there is now a requirement for development control decisions to accord with the development plan unless material considerations indicate otherwise. The detailed content of individual plan policies and proposals has therefore become even more important, for conservation as well as for other development plan topics.

1.5 Growing emphasis has been placed on the relationship between the different strands of conservation and the common thread of understanding, enjoyment, and access by the public. In 1993 the three conservation agencies worked together to produce *Conservation issues in strategic plans* (CCP 420). That document stressed the way that the remits of the three agencies spanned the full breadth of interest in England's cultural, historic, and natural environment - 'the great archaeological and historic legacy, the rich natural diversity of wildlife, the sense of place, character and identity of towns and villages, and the beauty and potential for enjoyment of the countryside'.

### Audience

1.6 This advice is aimed at those involved in preparing the new generation of district-wide local plans. It is also relevant to Part II of Unitary Development Plans and Mineral and Waste Plans. Many plans are of course already well advanced if not complete, and many have already used the advice in CCP 317. As the cycle continues plans will continue to be drafted, revised, published, and reviewed over the coming years. We hope this new advice will contribute ideas and information that will help at all of these stages and not just at the beginning of the process.

1.7 Many local plans already provide good coverage of our interests and we have drawn on these in providing examples of policies which demonstrate good practice. There is, however, considerable variation in the way that conservation topics are dealt with in plans and we see ample scope for improvement in policies and proposals. Through this advice our aim is to demonstrate what we would expect to find in plans which handle conservation topics well.

**Box 1.1 Planning Policy Guidance notes from the Department of the Environment**

PPG 1 General policy and principles
PPG 2 Green belts
PPG 3 Housing
PPG 4 Industrial and commercial development and small firms
PPG 5 Simplified planning zones
PPG 6 Major retail development
PPG 7 The countryside and the rural economy
PPG 8 Telecommunications
PPG 9 Nature conservation
[Nos. 10 and 11 are not in use at present]
PPG 12 Development plans and regional planning guidance
PPG 13 Transport
PPG 14 Development on unstable land
PPG 15 Planning and the historic environment
PPG 16 Archaeology and planning
PPG 17 Sport and recreation
PPG 18 Enforcing planning control
PPG 19 Outdoor advertisement control
PPG 20 Coastal planning
PPG 21 Tourism
PPG 22 Renewable energy
PPG 23 Planning and pollution control
PPG 24 Planning and noise

## Relationship to other documents and advice

1.8 For all planners the key source of advice is the series of Planning Policy Guidance notes produced by the Department of the Environment (DOE). These set out Government policy on a wide range of planning topics. The current series consists of the PPGs in Box 1.1.

There is also a Regional Planning Guidance series which provides advice on strategic planning and a Mineral Planning Guidance series, both of which are relevant.

1.9 Our aim is to complement the PPGs by giving more detailed consideration to conservation, access, and enjoyment issues. Where relevant and helpful we have summarised points of government policy to provide the context for our own advice. We have already produced guidance on a range of planning and conservation topics. These are referred to in notes throughout the text. The Countryside Commission's Countryside Planning File (CCP 452) is of general relevance and includes summaries of a wide range of planning advice.

1.10 This advice is written from the perspective of our conservation remits to complement government guidance as set out in PPGs. It does not replace, qualify or interpret the PPG notes which are issued by the Department of the Environment to set out Government policies on planning to be taken into account in preparing development plans and deciding planning applications.

## Local plans and other documents

1.11 Local plans are only one of a range of documents that local authorities are producing to indicate their approach to dealing with environmental issues and the interface with development. Many authorities are using a variety of non-statutory 'strategy' documents to cover these matters, partly in response to Government advice to exclude detailed consideration of implementation and management issues from local plans. These documents include countryside, nature conservation, urban heritage, recreation, and tourism strategies, which may cover these subjects either individually or in various combinations. In recent years there has also been growing emphasis on preparation of Local Agenda 21 strategies for sustainable development, often accompanied by State of the Environment reports and local Biodiversity Action Plans. These initiatives are encouraging local authorities to take a much broader environmental perspective on their activities and to seek much stronger integration of policies and practical action for the environment. In addition, new initiatives, for example the Countryside Design Summaries and Village Design Statements which are being promoted by the Countryside Commission, and urban archaeological strategies and Conservation Area appraisals promoted by English Heritage, will themselves result in additional documents which will operate alongside local plans.

1.12 Planning will be an increasingly important means of enabling and coordinating a wide range of activities concerned with the conservation and enhancement of the whole environment. It is therefore essential that local plans are carefully coordinated with this potentially wide range of other environmental documents, so that they support and reinforce rather than contradict each other. In many cases the non-statutory documents may need to become supplementary planning guidance to be read in association with the plan itself. Many of the new generation of environmental documents, notably Local Agenda 21 strategies, and more detailed ones like Village Design Statements, are being prepared in close consultation with, and often with the active involvement of, local communities. This level of community participation in matters affecting the local quality of life will increasingly raise expectations of consultation and community involvement in local planning. This means that special care will be needed to incorporate appropriate means of consultation and involvement in the plan preparation process.

## Format and content

1.13 This advice concentrates on the practical application of the general principles we believe should underpin the treatment of conservation issues as explored in detail in our advice on Strategic Plans (CCP 420). We do not repeat them in detail here, but summarise the main points in Chapter 2.

1.14 After this we focus on two areas, approaches to and policies for conserving and enhancing the environment (Part II) and the interface between conservation interests and the wide range of development or land use topics which must be addressed in local plans (Part III). Each of the main development topics is dealt with in a separate chapter.

1.15 In each section we follow a broadly similar format:

- a general introduction to the topic
- any specific government policies which apply
- a checklist of the specific subjects and policies which we would expect to see covered in plans
- a brief summary of our aims and objectives under each of these subject headings, together with an example policy demonstrating good practice, if available, and notes containing more detailed information and references

1.16 In selecting example policies for inclusion we have drawn on consultation draft, deposit draft, and adopted plans to find policies which best illustrate the approach advocated. We recognise that some draft policies may be amended as a result of local plan inquiries, but we have not found it helpful to restrict ourselves solely to policies in adopted plans. Wherever a policy is quoted we have indicated the status of the plan from which it is drawn.

1.17 We have not looked at all the plans currently available but have drawn on a sample of different types of plan. Not all of the example policies are perfect in their approach to our interests but we have selected them because they are moving in the right direction. Policies are constantly developing as experience grows and those we have selected are, in a sense, simply a 'snapshot' demonstrating the state of the art at a point in time.

1.18 As in previous advice we have in general deliberately refrained from using model policies, because we do not think that any one form of words is likely to be applicable in all circumstances. There are, however, one or two exceptions to this. Using example policies allows us to pass on ideas about good practice even though, in some cases, the wording may not be exactly as we would wish. Where we have not found a suitable policy on a particular topic we have usually omitted an example rather than include a model.

1.19 The wording of policies is especially important and there has been continuing debate about the best way of achieving both clarity and flexibility. The most recent advice from the DOE (summarised in a letter of 29 July 1994 sent to all County and District Planning Officers) is that use of the word 'normally' in policies is no longer advocated as a way of achieving flexibility. The preferred approach is to include objective criteria which clearly set out the circumstances in which planning permission will or will not be granted. Some of the policy examples we have used were drafted by planning authorities before this advice was issued, at a time when inclusion of 'normally' was still favoured. They should be read with this change of emphasis in mind.

# Chapter 2 General principles

## Introduction

2.1 *Conservation issues in strategic plans* (CCP 420) set out the general principles we believe should underpin the treatment of conservation issues in structure and regional plans. These principles are equally applicable to local plans and reference should be made to that document for a further discussion of the background. There are three key themes which are central to our approach:

- planning for sustainable development

- protecting natural resources and the non-renewable historic resource

- integration in planning for conservation

Each of these themes is briefly set out below. We then consider the practical implications for local plans.

## Planning for sustainable development

2.2 It is now widely recognised that land use planning must embrace the principles of sustainable development and there is a lively and continuing debate on how this can be achieved in practice. PPG 12, *Development plans and regional planning guidance,* emphasises the important role of the planning system and development plans in particular, in 'ensuring that development and growth are sustainable'. Our advice on strategic plans explored how plans could treat the issues of conservation, access, and enjoyment in a framework of sustainable development. Key points from this advice are summarised in Box 2.1, which sets down our current view of sustainable development and planning.

2.3 In 1994, the Government produced a statement of its own approach in *Sustainable development - The UK strategy* (COM 2426 HMSO 1994). This aims:

- to provide for the nation's needs for food production, minerals extraction, new homes, and other buildings, while respecting environmental objectives

- to use the already developed areas in the most efficient way, while making them more attractive places in which to live and work

- to conserve the natural resources of wildlife and landscape (safeguarding those identified as being of special interest or of national or international importance)

- to shape new development patterns in a way that minimises the use of energy consumed in travel between dispersed development

2.4 These aims focus on scenic and wildlife resources but it is now increasingly recognised that archaeological remains and other components of the historic environment are also a finite and irreplaceable resource and so must be given equal attention within the framework of planning for sustainable development. The aim should be to meet the needs of today without compromising the ability of future generations to understand, appreciate, and benefit from Britain's historic environment.

**Box 2.1 Our view of sustainable development**

We seek an environmentally led approach in all plans and consider this to be fundamental to achieving sustainable development. We recognise the great significance of the concept for our interests and the priority it deserves. The global consequences of the uncontrolled exploitation of raw materials and discharge of waste are now too serious to be ignored. As a result, governments throughout the world have endorsed the concept of sustainable development. This was usefully defined by the Brundtland Commission in 1987 as: '...development that meets the needs of the present generation without compromising the ability of future generations to meet their own needs.' The definition in the Government's white paper *This common inheritance: Britain's environmental strategy* carries the same message but is set in the terminology of the market place: '...(sustainable development) means living on the Earth's income rather than eroding its capital.'

There are now enough indicators of significant environmental change to justify a fundamental reassessment of our relationship with the natural and man-made environment. Both global and local imperatives encourage a change to sustainable development. In supporting this we have no wish to halt development, but rather to promote the right type of development at the right time and in the right place. Conservation and development are not alternatives, but are contrasting interests that must be reconciled and integrated within the concept of sustainable development. The planning system, properly used, can help to achieve this creative integration.

The strategic planning process can play a key part in moving society towards the idea of sustainable development. It cannot do so alone, nor should it try. It is a small but important factor in a much bigger equation, but a move to sustainable thinking, a growing understanding of conservation issues, and an emerging set of environmentally led policies will all contribute to the ultimate goal.

2.5 We have an interest in all these aspects of sustainable development and believe that both strategic and local plans have a vital role to play in moving society towards the idea. We believe that to do so planning authorities will need to address some key but sometimes unfamiliar concepts, in particular:

- the concept of environmental capacity

- the need for demand management

These two topics are considered in more detail below. The emphasis on sustainability also means that we must begin to consider much longer time horizons, looking at environmental consequences extending well beyond the life of a single plan.

**Environmental capacity**

2.6 Planning for sustainable development means making judgements about the ability of different environmental resources to cope with the demands upon them without unacceptable loss or damage. This leads to the concept of environmental capacity in which development thresholds are established. Thinking is still evolving on the way in which this concept applies to our different interests. It does, however, require that we distinguish two different types of environmental resources:

- the wider environment where there is a need to maintain the overall character and quality of the resource, but not necessarily its exact current make-up. Trading-off between environmental considerations and the needs of social and economic development may be acceptable, although a genuine balance of environmental resources should be maintained through appropriate compensatory measures (sometimes known as 'constant environmental assets').

- key natural and cultural resources that can be identified within this wider environment, which are considered vitally important and irreplaceable, and where any loss or damage would be extremely serious (sometimes known as 'critical environmental capital')

2.7 This distinction means that it is essential to identify and protect the key environmental resources of a plan area. These should include all resources identified as being of national importance, but also those of special importance in a more local context. It might also include sites of high potential, such as archaeological sites, the precise value of which cannot always be easily assessed. However, attention must be given, in the first instance, to characterising the wider environment and ensuring that its overall character and quality are maintained and enhanced. This division is reflected in the remainder of this advice, where we deal firstly with the wider environment (Chapter 3) and then with the special areas (Chapter 4).

**Demand management**

2.8 Plans will increasingly need to address ways in which demand for development can be modified rather than simply accommodated. Traditionally, the approach has been to forecast social and economic needs for land, for housing or industry, for new roads, for sites for waste disposal, and so on, and then to find land where they can be accommodated.

2.9 As we try to achieve sustainable development, with a greater emphasis on environmental concerns, it will become more difficult to accommodate needs defined in this way. We will need to find different ways of defining them, building on ideas about environmental capacity to define the scope for development in environmental terms. This will mean, for example, minimising waste through recycling, encouraging energy conservation, reducing the need to travel by careful location of new development, and so on.

## Protecting natural resources

2.10 Alongside our specific concerns for landscape, wildlife, and the historic environment, we recognise the global imperative of protecting the fundamental natural resources of air, water, and soil without which our more direct heritage conservation concerns would not exist. Policies for road transport and energy generation are central to such considerations because they are key causes of global warming, acid rain, and air pollution.

2.11 Because of their fundamental importance to sustainability, separate chapters of our advice explore the land use and environmental implications of transport (Chapter 8) and energy generation (Chapter 9). In the remainder of this section we concentrate on other aspects of protecting the natural resources of air, water, and soil, namely safeguarding quality (pollution control) and quantity.

**Air, water, and ground pollution**

2.12 The 1990 Government White Paper *This common inheritance* highlights the close relationship between pollution and land use. This is reinforced in PPG 23, *Planning and pollution control*, which advises that the planning system has an important role in determining the location of potentially polluting developments.

2.13 In local plans we would expect to see policy statements which:

- strongly support measures to improve current air and water quality

- strongly discourage polluting activities unless adequate controls can be imposed to ensure that harmful emissions and discharges are carefully contained

- pay particular attention to the protection of surface and groundwater resources which are susceptible to

**Box 2.2 Example policy on air, water, and ground pollution**

Warrington Borough Council includes the following policies in its 1994 Deposit Draft Local Plan:

**ENV 20:**
The Council will not permit development which is likely to cause direct harm by increasing levels of pollution through emissions into the air.

**ENV 23:**
The Council will not normally approve development which, in consultation with the National Rivers Authority, is considered likely to adversely affect the water quality of water bodies, their surface or waste water discharge, or the disturbance of contaminated land. The Council will generally support initiatives which lead to improvements in surface water quality.

**ENV 24:**
Developments will not be permitted which, in the opinion of the Council, after consultation with the National Rivers Authority, pose an unacceptable risk to the quality of groundwater.

a wide range of threats arising from land use policy (PPG 12, paragraph 6.19), including the surface and waste water discharge from developments, and the disturbance of contaminated land

2.14 Other policies within a local plan which may also have a bearing on pollution control include those relating to transport planning, energy generation, and minerals and waste disposal, with special reference to landfill.

**Protection of soil and water resources**
2.15 In the past, with strong emphasis on agricultural production, development plans laid stress on protecting the best and most versatile agricultural land (Grades 1, 2, and 3A) from irreversible loss to development. Although the imperative of agricultural production has now lessened we believe it remains important to protect the best of our soil resource, recognising that a global view of sustainability may, in the future, once again require greater emphasis on food production.

2.16 On the other hand, the availability of water has rarely been regarded as a planning constraint in England. Over-exploitation of certain water resources, notably the chalk and limestone aquifers of the south and east, contributes to the disappearance of some of our most attractive rivers and to low flows in many more, to the detriment of wildlife, landscape, and the setting of historic towns and villages. We therefore believe that the protection of the quality and quantity of water supply, and of river flows, must be regarded as a planning constraint when considering new development. This is considered further in Chapter 9 under the heading of water resources.

**Box 2.3 Integration of conservation and development issues**

Some general environmental and conservation considerations are common to all development topics, and merit special emphasis. They can be summarised as follows:

**Concern for all conservation interests**
In assessing the potential effects of development policies and proposals, the implications for all conservation interests (including landscape, wildlife, earth science, and archaeological, historical, and cultural features) need to be covered and given equal weight.

**Environmental capacity and demand management**
These concepts have already been discussed. Demand management can help to ensure that the environmental capacity of a plan area, however defined, is not exceeded by limiting some of the demands on it. If environmental capacity is reached, then demands can no longer be met without damage.

**The precautionary principle**
Full account must be taken of the 'precautionary principle', where there is uncertainty surrounding the environmental impacts of particular actions. In general, if there is uncertainty, then the action should be avoided unless or until its effects are more clearly understood. This might, for example, relate to areas where the balance of probability suggests, even in the absence of firm evidence, the existence of high conservation potential, such as hidden archaeological interest.

**Replacement value for environmental loss**
When essential development is likely to result in some environmental loss, there should be a principle, in addition to appropriate mitigation, for equivalent compensation by creation of new environmental resources, so that the overall character and quality of the environment are maintained in the long term. Archaeological remains and historic buildings are not replaceable on a like-for-like basis, and a translation of their replacement value into information value through recording can be only a poor substitute for the loss of historic fabric.

**Time-scale of environmental effects**
Our intention is to pass on to future generations an environment at least as valuable as today's, so we must consider the time-scale of environmental change. There is a particular need to consider longer time-scales, certainly beyond the life of a single plan.

## Integration in planning for conservation

2.17 Environmental and conservation considerations must not simply be confined to the chapter of the plan headed 'environment' or 'conservation'. Such wide issues need to be integrated into all aspects of local plans, permeating all the policies and proposals relating to individual development topics. This integrated way of thinking about environmental interests is critical in moving towards sustainable development. Some environmental and conservation considerations are common to all development topics and merit particular emphasis in local plans. The key ones are summarised in Box 2.3. Environmental appraisal of plans and policies is a key tool in achieving this form of integration.

2.18 The environmental and conservation issues arising from different types of development are considered in Part III of this advice. There are, however, a number of key general themes which are vitally important in planning for sustainable development and need to be given special emphasis. They relate to transport, the use of energy, non-renewable resources, the role of the urban fringe, and the importance of maintaining distinctiveness in the environment both nationally and locally: these are summarised in Box 2.4.

2.19 As the emphasis on sustainable development grows, there is also growing recognition of the need to integrate the different facets of conservation interests. Our own interests are increasingly intertwined, as is our shared interest in promoting understanding and enjoyment and facilitating access. We want to see this integration clearly reflected in local plans. We also recognise that on occasions our interests may not coincide and we are ready to help planning authorities to identify priorities if necessary.

2.20 In practical terms there will need to be growing emphasis on:

- coordinated approaches to state of the environment reports covering all our interests

- coordinated policies and proposals for maintaining and enhancing the character and quality of the wider environment in all its diversity

- strong and appropriate policies for safeguarding key environmental resources of all types

- integrated policies for promoting understanding and enjoyment and, where appropriate, facilitating access

**Box 2.4 Key themes in planning for sustainable development**

**Maintaining distinctiveness**
Variety and distinctiveness are among the most prized attributes of both our towns and countryside. Policies on conservation and enhancement and on different forms of development need to ensure that these qualities are maintained and that our surroundings do not become bland and homogenised. There is a need to maintain the individual and distinctive character of towns and villages and of landscapes and habitats both at the large scale, looking at England as a whole, and at the local level.

**Transport**
Road transport is a major contributor to environmental concerns. The forecast increases in the number of motor vehicles are a major threat to the environment, both directly, in terms of congestion, fuel consumption, noise, vibration, and air pollution, and indirectly, through the requirement for new roads and use of raw materials for making vehicles. The direct effects are a special concern in historic towns and where traffic impinges on the tranquillity and character of the countryside. Particular emphasis must be given in plans to reducing the number of journeys by cutting down the need to travel, developing integrated transport and land use plans, and using traffic management measures in town and country. These considerations have major consequences for the location of new development, influencing, for example, the choice between in town/edge of town locations for retail development.

**The urban fringe**
The urban fringe, or the countryside around towns, will have an increasingly important role to play as sustainable approaches to land use planning are developed. These areas can make the countryside easily accessible, reducing the need to travel; they can also provide opportunities for enhancing derelict and degraded land and scope for compensatory green areas to minimise pollution and improve air quality. Special policies are needed to encourage the conservation, enhancement, appropriate use, and enjoyment of these important areas in ways which do not encourage urban sprawl and encroachment into rural areas.

**Energy**
Policies for energy conservation are important for the contribution they can make to a number of environmental objectives including reduction in greenhouse gases. We place particular emphasis on promoting energy conservation, sensitive development of renewable energy sources, and the need to find more energy-efficient patterns of land use and development, again influencing location of development such as homes, shops, and offices.

**Non-renewable resources**
The use of non-renewable resources, especially minerals, has major planning implications. We stress the use of environmental capacity to establish acceptable limits to mineral extraction and reduction of demand for primary minerals both by recycling and by influencing the design of development to limit demand.

**Box 2.5 Example of keynote environmental policy and supporting rationale**

Hambleton District Council includes the following policy in its 1994 Deposit Draft District-wide Local Plan.

GS1:
All development must take full account of the need to protect the environment so that present-day demands do not compromise the ability of future generations to meet their own needs or enjoy a high quality environment. All development must reflect the need to safeguard and improve the quality of life of residents, conserve energy resources, and protect and, where possible, enhance the Plan area's essential character and main environmental assets such as:

- the Howardian Hills AONB and the Nidderdale AONB
- the general attractiveness and diversity of the landscape
- the open and undeveloped nature of the countryside
- the York Green Belt
- areas of wildlife and ecological value
- the setting, form and character of settlements
- the quality of air supplies
- the quality of streams, rivers, and groundwater
- high quality agricultural land
- buildings and areas of special townscape, historic, and architectural interest
- sites of archaeological importance
- land of recreation and amenity value
- the public rights-of-way network

The importance of environmental considerations in maintaining and improving the quality of life is now widely recognised and the environment is more than ever a fundamental concern of planning. The Planning and Compensation Act 1991 requires that local plans include policies for the conservation of the natural beauty and amenity of the land and policies for the improvement of the physical environment, and PPG 12 advises that policies should be in line with the concept of sustainable development.

**Box 2.6 Steps in planning for sustainable development**

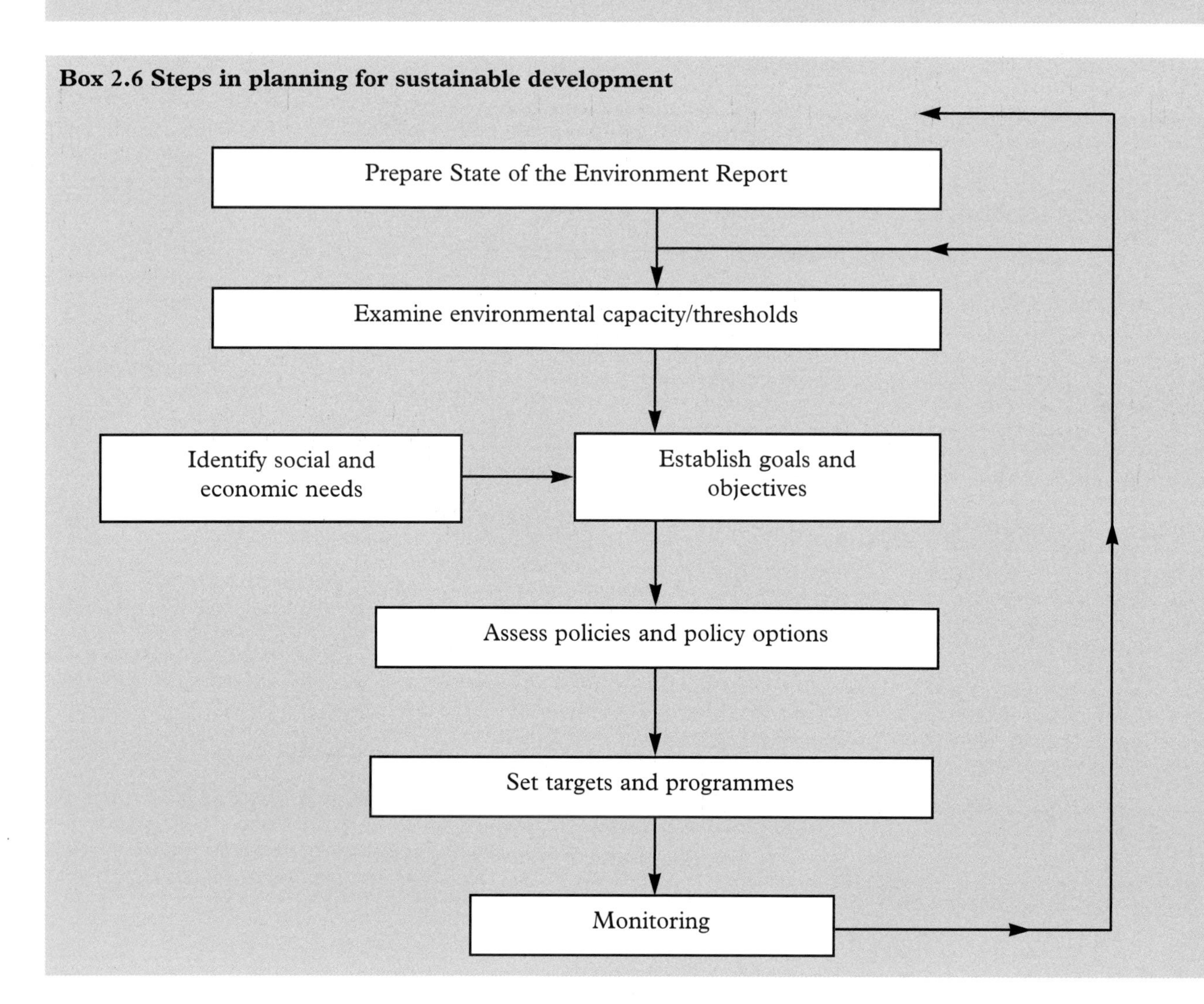

## Practical implications for local plans

2.21 Much that has been written about sustainable development is at a theoretical level, but planners need practical help with the tasks that they must achieve. We set out below some more practical pointers on:

- environmentally led plans
- methods of plan preparation which emphasise environmental interests
- guidance which will influence the nature of development proposals

**Environmentally led plans**
2.22 Environmentally led local plans are, in our view, most likely to be able to deliver sustainable development. The prominence of environmental considerations needs to be clearly signalled by setting out, at the beginning of the plan, the environmental rationale upon which it is based and the environmental and other objectives which the plan seeks to meet. As part of this statement there should be a keynote environmental policy setting out general environmental criteria against which all new development proposals will be judged. This policy should show what the local authority is trying to achieve through the plan, perhaps with reference to other related local authority initiatives.

2.23 The rationale, and the keynote policy with its criteria, should make it clear that all conservation interests, including landscape, wildlife, earth science, and archaeological, historical, and cultural features, will be taken into account in considering development proposals. Such a policy should then either be repeated, or prominently referred to, at the start of every development topic.

2.24 Though plans will increasingly (as in Paragraph 2.8) find ways to reduce the need for new development, significant demands will remain to be met. In making decisions about ways of accommodating necessary development, account should be taken of environmental capacity as well as potential consequences for the full range of environmental and conservation interests. Account must also be taken of the environmental considerations set out in Box 2.3. Carrying out a strategic environmental appraisal of plans and policies is the best way of ensuring that all these factors are fully taken into account. This approach is described in paragraphs 2.34 and 2.35.

**Methods of plan preparation**
2.25 Our advice on strategic plans (CCP 420) set out an approach to preparing plans which is geared to the requirements of sustainable development. This approach is summarised in Box 2.6. We fully recognise that local authorities are in many different stages of plan preparation and review and may not be able to change their approach at this stage. However, we hope that as the cycle of plan review continues this approach will become more common over time. We place particular emphasis on:

- preparing State of the Environment Reports
- examining environmental capacity and defining key environmental resources
- assessing policies, policy options, and proposals for their environmental consequences

**State of the Environment Reports**
2.26 There is a growing trend for local authorities to produce State of the Environment Reports dealing with all aspects of the environment of their area. These aim both to describe the current state of the environment and to provide a basis for action and for monitoring. Though the environmental baseline required for local plans may not be quite as all-embracing as these wider reports, a report on the different components of the environment of the plan area will still provide an essential starting point for preparing plans.

2.27 A State of the Environment Report should set out, for the full range of environmental topics:

- the present state of knowledge and any gaps in the information
- trends in environmental quality
- indicators of environmental quality which can be used in monitoring

2.28 In terms of our own interests we would expect such a report to identify, characterise, and evaluate as appropriate, landscape, wildlife habitats, earth science interests, archaeological, historical, and cultural features (including areas of potential interest where further survey is necessary, and recognising the high degree of uncertainty relating to archaeology), and the range of opportunities for access and enjoyment. As far as possible there should be some assessment of the pressures which are affecting these resources, and their vulnerability to change. In short, such reports should be concerned with the whole environment.

2.29 Each of us has a growing interest in characterising and describing environmental resources, and new techniques are emerging and evolving. We are collaborating on national initiatives (see Box 2.7) which will provide a context for the more detailed assessments which local authorities will be involved in, particularly:

- the Countryside Commission's 'Countryside Character Programme' which identifies and analyses regional diversity in our landscapes

**Box 2.7 A common strategic framework**

All three agencies are embarking on major strategic programmes, broadly linked by the idea of landscape character. The programme, both jointly and individually, will lead to a framework for promoting the interests of the agencies and setting strategic objectives. The programmes have different purposes, timescales, and applications but they also have much in common. Accordingly, close connections are being made between the three approaches, including the preparation of a joint Regional Character Map as a common framework for all.

The Countryside Commission's Countryside Character Programme will provide a comprehensive understanding of the character of the English landscape. It will have three interlocking components:

- a national map will divide the country into a series of areas of cohesive landscape character, viewed from a regional perspective
- a series of analytical landscape descriptions which are linked to the map
- regional landscape strategies which will indicate broad aspirations for the English countryside, and opportunities to conserve and enhance its character

English Nature's Natural Areas Programme will provide a framework for integrating work on conserving the natural heritage. 'Natural Area' is not a designation; it denotes a district with a distinctive character, reflecting its typical plants, animals, land forms, and land use, and their interactions with people over time. English Nature has, through consultation, produced a map of England's 116 Natural Areas, including maritime areas. In six pilot Natural Areas English Nature has been working with local groups to see how the concept can help coordinate sustaining and enhancing local wildlife and natural features.

English Heritage's Historic Landscape Programme includes:

- research on methods of assessing historic landscape. A number of exemplars are in preparation at a county or similar level. English Heritage has prepared maps of settlement and field patterns as part of the joint Regional Character Map and it has also commissioned a detailed map and characterisation of historic, traditional settlement regions.
- the Monuments at Risk Survey (MARS), which will identify the type, location, distribution, and condition of archaeological sites ('monuments'). This will, for the first time, allow an archaeological characterisation of landscape areas or regions in a manner similar to Natural Areas.

---

- English Heritage's work on identifying and characterising the historic landscape and on quantifying the condition and scale of the country's archaeological and built heritage (MARS)
- English Nature's work on describing and setting objectives for 'Natural Areas' throughout the country. Our agencies also provide technical advice and support for more detailed work by local authorities.

2.30 The aim should be a steady progression towards a comprehensive baseline, as resources allow. Many different sources of existing information can be drawn on, including:

- habitat surveys and biological records held by County Councils, County Wildlife Trusts, other voluntary wildlife groups, museums, biological records centres, the London Ecology Unit, the National Rivers Authority, and English Nature
- landscape assessments carried out by County Councils, the National Rivers Authority, the Countryside Commission, or others (including, for example, Community Forest Teams)
- the local authority Sites and Monuments Records (SMRs), normally held and maintained by the County Councils, which contain information on archaeological sites and, in some cases, historic buildings, and maps of archaeological constraints, including areas of archaeological potential, which county archaeologists may have produced
- the statutory list of buildings of special architectural and historic interest, any local lists of important buildings, information on Conservation Areas, and local or national registers of buildings at risk
- the English Heritage Register of Historic Parks and Gardens and additional information held by counties or districts on locally important sites
- the English Heritage register of historic battlefields
- information about World Heritage Sites
- information assembled by counties and districts on access land, rights of way, and other informal opportunities for recreation
- information assembled by parish and community councils or local groups, including parish maps, village appraisals, village design statements, and other similar studies

2.31 Conservation interests are increasingly interlinked and we therefore want to emphasise the need for information and new surveys on these topics to be integrated and coordinated as much as possible. Thus, for example, landscape assessment should embrace the historic dimension of the landscape, nature conservation assessments should reflect the earth science and archaeological interest of semi-natural habitats, and townscape or conservation area assessments should also take account of archaeological or wildlife interests.

**Environmental capacity and key environmental resources**

2.32 Consideration of environmental capacity will be a key step in the process. The approach will depend on the environmental resource being considered. In terms of landscape, definition of capacity is not likely to be absolute, because the concern is generally with large areas which will inevitably experience some change and where a complete 'hands off' approach is unlikely to be appropriate. For wildlife habitats and some important archaeological sites the constraints will be firmer. There will always be difficult decisions to be made, however, especially in rural areas where it is important to achieve the integration of development which is essential to support local communities and conservation of the environment.

2.33 Nevertheless, an environmentally led approach to local plans will require clear definition of both the key environmental resources that will be firmly protected from development, and the character and quality of the wider environment which will be maintained and enhanced.

The character and quality of the wider environment should be fully described, identifying the features which are of greatest importance in contributing to this and which should be maintained and enhanced.

Key environmental resources should be identified and mapped on the proposals map, including some reference to areas of potential importance which cannot yet be fully defined. Important landscapes, wildlife habitats, earth science features, and archaeological and historical features (where they can be adequately defined) should be included. They may be important at any level from local to national.

**Assessing policies and proposals for their environmental consequences**

2.34 There may be a number of different ways of meeting the objectives of a plan, working within agreed environmental limits, leading to a number of different alternative options for policies and plan proposals. The environmental effects of these alternatives need to be carefully assessed before final decisions are reached on the preferred approach.

2.35 We fully support the use of environmental appraisal in the process of local plan preparation and believe that it is fundamental to integrated planning aimed at achieving sustainable development. We welcome the statement in PPG 12 calling for the systematic appraisal, as part of the plan preparation process, of the environmental implications of policies and policy options, and also the Department of the Environment's publication of practical advice on how local authorities can achieve this (*The environmental appraisal of development plans - a good practice guide*, DOE 1993, ISBN 0-11-752866-8, HMSO, £10). This advice is a welcome first step towards encouraging local authorities to take seriously the requirement that they should consider as fully as possible the environmental implications of what they are proposing.

2.36 The DOE advice does not give specific support to the approach to environmental capacity and the definition of different types of environmental resources that we are advocating, but the DOE has promised further national guidance on ways of incorporating the requirements of sustainable development into the planning process. In the meantime, we believe that the most important thing is that those responsible for producing local plans should give the fullest possible consideration to the potential environmental consequences of what they are proposing.

**Influencing the nature of development proposals**

2.37 Local plans should also include policies which will help to influence the nature of development proposals. Some guidance on this is given in the PPG series, especially in PPG 16 dealing with archaeology. Four topics merit particular attention in terms of our interests, namely:

- design of new development
- requirements for environmental assessment environmental benefits
- planning obligations

**Design of new development**

2.38 There is growing recognition of the importance of good design in maintaining and enhancing the character and quality of the environment. This applies at all scales in all locations, including, for example, new commercial development in town centres, infill housing in rural villages, and the conversion of individual farm buildings in the countryside. The government has expressed its commitment to good design in PPG 1, especially in Annex A, which indicates the potential scope of development plan policies on design. The DOE has published a discussion document, *Quality in town and country,* which considers design issues. It is also carrying out research on this topic and will be issuing, in due course, a good practice guide on local plan policies on design. In addition, the Countryside Commission has published advice on the principles of design in the countryside and is preparing detailed guidance on the production of Countryside Design Summaries and Village Design Statements.

2.39 Local plans should stress the need for a high standard of design in all new development, not just in special areas. New development ought to respect the harmony and the existing traditional relationships between buildings, settlement, and the landscape, in terms of landscape character and local distinctiveness, the character of the urban environment, the historical and cultural elements of the environment, and wildlife habitats and earth science features. Special attention needs to be given to the scale and density of development, the size, form, and grouping of buildings, and the relationship of materials and design to local vernacular character.

2.40 Plans should give guidance on design matters and refer, where appropriate, to any supplementary design guidance. Specific advice may be needed on different aspects of the built environment, dealing for example with choice of materials, the special sensitivity of conservation areas and listed buildings, buildings in the countryside, and new development in different types of urban area.

2.41 Perhaps most importantly, policies and supporting guidance should be based on a thorough and, as far as possible, shared understanding of the character of the local landscape and of towns and villages, of the individual characteristics that make each area distinctive and of the harmony between settlements and the landscape. Landscape assessments, townscape appraisals, conservation area assessments, countryside design summaries, and village design statements are the types of practical tool that will assist in this. Local authorities should demonstrate in plans their commitment to using these tools in making decisions about development. In some local plans it may be appropriate to be more specific about design requirements for certain key areas of development. A policy can be included which states that design briefs will be prepared for such key areas, and which describes the factors that might be covered in such a brief.

**Box 2.8 Example policy on design**

Hambleton District Council includes the following policy in its 1994 Deposit Draft, District-wide Local Plan.

BD2:
Development proposals in the countryside should respect the diversity and distinctiveness of local landscape character. In towns and villages, proposals should relate to the context provided by buildings, street and plot patterns, building frontages, topography, established public views, landmark buildings, and other townscape elements. Proposals which do not respect the local context or the scale, height, proportion, and materials of surrounding buildings and development which constitutes over-development of the site by virture of scale, height or bulk will not normally be permitted.

**Requirements for environmental assessment**

2.42 Statutory regulations set out the types of development that may formally require an environmental assessment, though there can be variation in the way that the regulations are applied, depending on local circumstances. Local plans should not simply repeat the regulations, but should contain a policy which indicates, specifically for their area, the types of development where an environmental assessment is likely to be required, in what areas, and the types of environmental effect that will need specifically to be covered.

2.43 Such policies might usefully refer to the need for such assessments where:

- key environmental resources, as described above, are likely to be affected
- other sensitive areas which are of a particularly significant character or quality for their landscape, wildlife, earth science or archaeological, historical, and cultural features (or a combination of these) are likely to be affected
- the development in question is of a new type where there is uncertainty about the possible environmental consequences.

2.44 In setting out the environmental effects that should be covered, policies will need to stress the timescale of possible environmental effects, ensuring that both long-term and short-term effects are addressed. They should also refer to the importance of the 'precautionary principle' and the need to identify areas where there is uncertainty surrounding the environmental consequences of a particular development. This may be important where the development is new, or where there is incomplete environmental information, for example in areas of hidden archaeological interest or potential. In the latter case it will be essential to determine the archaeological potential and survival of an area before reaching final decisions about development, as required by PPG 16.

**Environmental benefits and planning obligations**

2.45 There are opportunities for many forms of development to contribute positively to environmental enhancement. If development is likely to result in some environmental loss, and once all practicable steps have been taken to mitigate the adverse effects, then there should be an attempt to secure appropriate compensation for this by the creation of new environmental resources, so that the overall character and quality of the environment are maintained in the long term. Special problems do, however, arise with archaeological resources and other historic features such as ancient woodlands, where any loss is absolute because such features are either irreplaceable or, in the case of habitats, could be recreated only over very long timescales.

2.46 Though there are other mechanisms, compensation or enhancement are increasingly being achieved by means of planning obligations under the provisions of Section 106 of the Town and Country Planning Act 1990 and the Planning and Compensation Act 1991. Government guidance on the use of planning obligations is set out in Circular 16/91 and in PPG 12 and makes it clear that the benefit which is being sought must be reasonable both in scale and kind. Such benefits must be related to the development and necessary to the granting of planning permission. In general obligations can offer a broader basis for environmental and other benefits than normal planning conditions.

2.47 Whatever the benefits that can be gained, there are no circumstances where development should be justified solely by this potential. Environmental benefits cannot justify a development that is fundamentally unsound, nor should they influence the allocation of land in a local plan or be used to justify projects that are in conflict with adopted plans. Decisions on development proposals must be made solely on the basis of sound planning policies and criteria. Care must also be taken to ensure that any decline or deterioration in land or buildings, in anticipating Section 106 agreements, does not become an argument in favour of development.

2.48 However, when acceptable development proposals are put forward it should be good practice for all involved to explore the potential for securing benefits for the environment. Local plans should include a policy setting out expectations of planning obligations. This might usefully set down the types of development, or the specific locations where benefits will be sought, the types of benefit considered appropriate, either in general or for specific sites, and the mechanisms that will be used to secure them. Obligations can be sought which will help to maintain or preserve amenity or provide benefits to offset environmental impacts or losses.

2.49 The types of potential environmental benefit that might be included in such policies are:

- landscape benefits, including more generous landscape treatment, and sensitive planting and management of trees and shrubs, provided that it takes account of archaeological resources, and is in keeping with the character of the area

- protection, restoration, repair, and management of important features such as trees, woodlands, and boundary features like walls or hedges

- creation or restoration of appropriate wildlife habitats such as ponds, wetland, meadows, and woodland, with appropriate access provision

- the protection and repair or reuse of historic buildings, features of historic landscape interest or archaeological remains, with provision for access and interpretation if appropriate

- enhanced provision for access and enjoyment, including new footpaths, cycleways, and bridleways, open space such as informal parks, community woodland, meadows or pocket parks, and support or provision of facilities such as visitor centres or information and interpretation

2.50 The list of benefits sought, and the circumstances in which they will be pursued, should not be so extensive or inflexible that they will inhibit developers from coming forward with schemes for negotiation. They should also reflect government advice in Circular 16/91 and in PPG 12. The Countryside Commission has issued a separate policy statement *Countryside benefits from planning obligations* (1994) which includes practical examples of their use and the DOE publication *Development Plans - a good practice guide* (1992) gives some hypothetical examples of policies but does not specifically mention environmental benefits.

2.51 Clear thinking about the impacts of development on the environment, about reasonable compensation for this, and about realistic enhancement opportunities, should guide formulation of policies for local plans.

# PART II CONSERVING AND ENHANCING THE ENVIRONMENT

## Chapter 3 Conserving and enhancing the character and quality of the environment

### Introduction

3.1 In Chapter 2 we outlined the general principles underpinning our approach to conservation issues in local plans. Central to these principles is the need to distinguish between, and to develop appropriate policies for, both the whole of the wider environment and the more specific key natural and cultural resources. This chapter deals with the first of these to provide a comprehensive framework for the special areas considered in Chapter 4. In reading both chapters it is very important to remember that we fully accept that new sustainable development is necessary in both town and country: the task for planners is to devise policies which will result in the right type of development, in the right location, built in a way which is in keeping with its surroundings and which makes a positive contribution to the character and quality of its surroundings.

3.2 The wider environment offers some of the greatest opportunities for integrating conservation interests. The importance of a rich, diverse, and healthy environment in both town and country is now widely recognised. Maintaining and enhancing this complex environment means taking an integrated view of characteristic landscapes, wildlife habitats, geological and geomorphological features, archaeology, historic features, buildings, and settlements. It is the combination of all of these that contributes so much to variety and sense of place in our surroundings.

3.3 In seeking to maintain and enhance the wider environment we want local plans to include policies and proposals which are aimed at the rural and urban environment.

### The rural environment

3.4 In rural areas the aim of planning must be to sustain an attractive, diverse, high-quality, accessible, thriving, and environmentally healthy countryside. The historic fabric of buildings, archaeological features, historic parks and gardens, and the wider historic landscape, together with wildlife and geological and land form features, all need to be protected and enhanced.

3.5 We encourage policies that are designed to achieve these aims by giving attention not just to special environmental resources, but also to the more commonplace things around us. This means understanding what makes one area different from another (but not necessarily more or less valuable) – the character of the landscape, the typical features, the wildlife habitats and the types of insects, birds, and animals, and the great depth of history which can be read in the landscape and in its buildings and settlements. Carefully constructed policies are needed to make sure that all the things people value in their surroundings are taken fully into account in reaching planning decisions.

**Box 3.1 Local plan checklist for the rural environment**

We expect local plans to contain policies aimed at:

- conserving and enhancing the diversity and distinctiveness of landscape character in the plan area, with evidence that this is based on the appropriate use of landscape assessment
- conserving and enhancing the historic landscape
- recognising the importance of the full range of wildlife habitats with appropriate policies to protect them
- protecting important features in the countryside, including trees, hedges, walls, and archaeological, geological or geomorphological features
- ensuring that the important contribution of historic and characteristic buildings, settlements, and historic parks and gardens to the countryside is maintained and enhanced
- supporting the enhancement of landscapes and habitats and, where appropriate, the creation of new ones

#### Landscape diversity and distinctiveness

3.6 Landscape is an important and highly valued part of the environmental resource of every district. It contributes greatly to the identity of an area, provides the setting for day-to-day life, contributes to the economy because of its role in attracting tourism and business, and is often a source of enjoyment and inspiration. Virtually all landscape, however unassuming, means something special to someone.

3.7 It is still necessary to have policies to protect certain landscapes which are considered, for whatever reason, to be of outstanding importance, either

**Box 3.2 Example policy on conserving and enhancing landscape character**

Doncaster Unitary Development Authority includes the following policy in its 1994 Deposit Draft Local Plan:

ENV 18:
The Borough Council will promote the conservation and enhancement of the Borough's landscape and seek to maintain local variations in that landscape. Wherever possible, woodlands, grasslands, and other habitats of landscape importance together with valuable existing landscape features, such as hedgerows, trees, copses, ponds, watercourses, historical sites, estate features, enclosure landscapes, stone walls, and other built heritage features will be protected and enhanced.

nationally or at a more local level. Advice on this is given in Chapter 4. Increasingly, however, the emphasis in plans should be on landscape character – what makes one landscape different from another, rather than what makes it better or worse. This allows policies to be directed towards maintaining diversity and distinctiveness of landscape character. It means that more time and resources will need to be devoted to understanding and explaining what gives an area its particular character.

3.8 Plans should contain policies to ensure that development proposals and land use allocations respect the special character and quality of the surrounding landscape and the features that contribute to this. To achieve this aim effectively there should be a summary description in the plan of the landscape character of the plan area, based on landscape assessment.

3.9 Once landscape character has been described, it can provide a point of reference for many aspects of planning policy, as well as for detailed development control decisions. Often it will be necessary to go further than this and to decide on the appropriate overall strategy for each landscape type or area. A useful approach is to divide such strategies into one of two broad categories:

***Conservation*** A conservation strategy is appropriate for landscapes of strong and distinctive character which are highly valued for their special qualities and sense of place, often based on retention of traditional landscape character. Some of these areas may be nationally designated as National Parks, AONBs or Heritage Coasts. Others may be more appropriately defined as Special Landscape Areas in local plans. Emphasis will need to be given to conservation of the special character and quality of these areas.

***Enhancement*** An enhancement strategy is appropriate where landscape character is becoming weakened, individual features have suffered significant decline or damage, and positive improvement is needed. Enhancement can take three forms:

- restoration to repair landscapes which still have a reasonably intact character but where there is a decline in condition
- reconstruction to recreate an earlier landscape which has been to a large extent lost, though this raises difficult questions about whether earlier landscapes can or should be recreated
- creation to form a new and different landscape, in keeping with its surroundings, where little of value survives

3.10 Where the landscape is particularly important for its historic character, strategies of enhancement are less likely to be appropriate. Special care then needs to be taken to understand the 'palimpsest', the layers of history which form the historic environment in its widest sense. There may still, however, be a need to enhance individual features which may be in decline, for example eroded hedgerow patterns.

***Notes***
*There is reference to the use of the systematic assessment of landscape character in preparing development plans in PPG 7, paragraph 1.14, and in PPG 15, paragraph 6.40.*

*Advice on methods of landscape assessment is contained in the Countryside Commission's 1993 publication* Landscape assessment guidance *(CCP 423) and also, for river landscapes, in the National Rivers Authority's 1993 report* River landscape assessment *(Conservation Technical Handbook No. 2).*

*Further discussion of policies for locally designated 'special' landscapes is included in Chapter 4.*

*The Countryside Commission's Countryside Character Programme is designed to describe diversity in landscape character from a regional perspective. It will provide a context for more local assessments.*

**The historic landscape**
3.11 As well as its scenic character and quality, the landscape which surrounds us has equal value for its historic and archaeological dimensions. Human interaction with nature over many thousands of years has left innumerable visible traces in the English landscape. This legacy is finite, irreplaceable, and non-renewable. It includes complex patterns and interrelationships of individual archaeological sites, historic parkland, settlement remains, ancient woodland, field patterns with their associated hedges or walls, enclosure systems, trackways, and industrial remains, and allows us to read much about our origins and history in the fabric of the landscape. The presence of the past within today's countryside is increasingly being valued as a very significant aspect of the rural environment, and is emphasised, for example, by PPG 15 in paragraph 6.20.

**Box 3.3 Example policy on conserving and enhancing the historic landscape**

Cotswold District Council includes the following policy in its 1994 proposed changes to the Deposit Draft Local Plan:

POLICY 24:
1 Development will not be permitted which would destroy, damage or adversely affect the character, appearance or setting of an historic landscape, or of any if its features, including parks and gardens of special historic interest.

2 Schemes to improve, restore, and manage the historic landscape will be sought in connection with, and commensurate with the scale of, any new development affecting an historic landscape.

3.12 It is important to recognise that, just as all landscape may be valued by someone, so all landscape is to a greater or lesser extent historic. This recognition needs to influence the overall approach to the rural environment. One of the best ways to take account of the historic dimension of the landscape is to build a concept of historic landscape character into the process of landscape assessment. Scenic landscape character can then be clearly linked to its historic origins. The value of individual features can also be judged not only in terms of their contribution to the appearance of the landscape, but also of their importance as part of the historical 'palimpsest', providing evidence of our past and one of the reasons why we value our surroundings. Such full assessments will inform local plan policies and provide a basis for supplementary planning guidance or rural strategies.

3.13 Many local plans currently confine their attention to known archaeological sites, historic buildings or historic parks and gardens. A few take the lead from structure plans and contain policies for ancient landscapes or for areas of historic interest, or other similar categories. Planning authorities should now take a more comprehensive view of the historic landscape. This is a developing subject where thinking is likely to evolve further and approaches to the description, classification, and, if appropriate, evaluation of the historic landscape are in the early stages of development. An approach that we particularly encourage consists of:

- characterisation and assessment of the historic dimension of the landscape of local plan areas, for instance by extending the scope and methods of landscape assessment, by special studies of individual areas, and as part of State of the Environment Reports
- drafting of policies which seek to protect the historic fabric and character of the landscape, ensure that any proposals for development do not have a significant adverse impact on it and are in sympathy with the past, and, where appropriate, enhance its condition
- identification of any aspects of the landscape which are of special historic interest and which merit more detailed attention in considering proposals for development or change in land use

3.14 PPG 15 gives support, in paragraph 6.40, to this general approach to appraising the wider historic landscape. It indicates that assessment of the historic character of the whole countryside is likely to be more flexible and more effectively integrated with the aims of the planning process than an attempt to define selected areas for additional control. In adopting this approach to the wider countryside planning authorities may sometimes wish to work together to consider historic landscape character at a larger scale beyond the confines of their own area.

***Notes***

This common inheritance, *the 1990 White Paper on the environment, drew attention to the topic of historic landscapes, and English Heritage subsequently produced a policy statement on the subject in 1991. Its 1992 leaflet* Development plan policies for archaeology *indicated that historic landscapes were a suitable topic for inclusion in plans. Since then English Heritage has been involved in a programme of research to test a variety of approaches. Further guidance and advice may arise from this.*

*The Countryside Commission has published a draft policy statement,* Views from the past, *on historic landscape character. Helpful information is also contained in the Council for British Archaeology policy statement* The past in tomorrow's landscape *(1993).*

**Wildlife habitats**

3.15 As PPG 9 notes in paragraph 14, our wildlife heritage is not confined to statutorily designated areas. In addition to the sites which have been formally recognised for their nature conservation value (dealt with in Chapter 4), many areas contain a rich mosaic of wildlife habitats. These include all types of unimproved grassland such as chalk downland or neutral grassland, wetlands, coastal habitats, lowland heath, and upland habitats such as heather or grass moorland, as well as features such as reservoirs, canals, road verges, and areas of wasteland. These

**Box 3.4 Example policy on protecting semi-natural habitats**

Hambleton District Council include the following policy in its 1994 Deposit Draft, District Wide Local Plan:

NC6:
Where appropriate, semi-natural habitats important for nature conservation such as ancient semi-natural woodland, heathlands, unimproved grassland, ponds, and other wetland features will be protected from any development which may adversely affect their value for nature conservation.

habitats have nature conservation value both in their own right and as corridors, links or stepping stones joining one habitat to another. In addition, they often contribute to the character of the landscape, as well as being part of the historical and archaeological fabric of the landscape and highly valued by local communities.

3.16 In keeping with PPG 9, which in turn reflects the EC Habitats Directive, local plans need to include policies to encourage the management of features which are of importance for wild flora and fauna. The degree of protection afforded to these habitats and features outside designated areas will depend on their degree of importance.

***Notes***
*It will usually be desirable to have a separate policy for non-designated habitats, though sometimes a combined policy, linking designated sites and other habitats together, may be appropriate.*

*If not covered elsewhere, such policies should also make reference to the mitigation of damage, if necessary by habitat re-creation, in the event that damaging development does have to be permitted.*

*English Nature has been testing the value of the Natural Area concept in helping to coordinate efforts to sustain and enhance local wildlife and natural features.*

## Important features in the countryside

3.17 A wide range of individual features is of particular importance in contributing to the character and quality of the countryside, most notably trees and woodlands, traditional field boundaries (such as hedges, hedgerows, hedgebanks, dykes, and walls) and boundary patterns, and historic designed parkland and gardens. Such features have a vital role in the landscape, provide highly visible evidence of the historical evolution of the landscape, and are important for wildlife.

3.18 Policies should be included which recognise the importance of such features and protect them from the adverse effects of development. These features raise different issues and will often merit separate policies, although with careful wording combined policies may be appropriate.

### Trees and woodlands

3.19 Trees and woodlands are one of the most widely valued parts of our environment in both town and country, with their cultural and historical associations, their importance for nature conservation, and their contribution to the landscape. Local plans should contain a strong commitment to protecting them from development or other damaging change, if necessary by the use of Tree Preservation Orders, especially where they are in one or more of the following categories:

- ancient woodland, identified by English Nature as woodlands which have existed from at least medieval times without ever having been cleared for uses other than wood or timber production
- important tree and woodland features contributing to the character of open spaces in or near settlements, or in the wider landscape, including those associated with major road routes, with rivers, lakes, and canals, or in highly visible positions

**Box 3.5 Example policy on protection of trees and woodlands**

Wealden District Council includes the following policy in its 1995 Deposit Local Plan:

EN21:
The Council will seek to retain and enhance the contribution of trees and woodland areas to the landscape character of the district. Particular regard will be given to the High and Low Weald, the setting of settlements, and the amenity value of trees within built-up areas. This will be promoted by:

- endorsement of the principles and guidelines contained in the Trees and Woodland Strategy for East Sussex
- support for the preparation of local Trees and Woodland Conservation and Management Plans
- encouragement for woodland management and participation in tree and hedgerow planting schemes by farmers, voluntary organisations and others
- making Tree Preservation Orders where appropriate to protect trees and woodland areas of significant amenity value
- a sympathetic approach to enterprises that help sustain and manage forestry and woodland areas
- resisting development proposals which would result in the loss of trees which make a valuable contribution to the character of the landscape, a settlement or its setting

3.20 The management of trees and woodlands is often as important as their protection. Though not a wholly appropriate subject for land use and development policies, except as indicated by the EC Habitats Directive (see paragraph 3.16 above), issues relating to the management of trees and woodlands may usefully be covered in the supporting text or justification. Here attention could be given briefly to the use of indicative forestry strategies, to the importance of managing existing woodlands and to the way in which local authorities may respond to consultations on forestry matters.

***Notes***
*Government guidance on the use of Indicative Forestry*

*Strategies is contained in DoE Circular 29/92. This circular also explains the relationship between these strategies and development plans.*

*The Countryside Commission has published its policies on trees and woodlands in the publication* England's trees and woods *(CCP 408, 1993).*

**Fields and field boundaries**

3.21 In many rural areas the distinctive type of field boundary, as well as the pattern of fields enclosed, is the most dominant feature of the landscape and the most obvious reminder of past patterns of historic land use and management.

PPG 15 (paragraph 6.2) recognises the importance of these features within the historic environment. Sometimes it may be helpful to include a separate policy on the protection of such features, although they can also be included in a general policy that embraces other features as well.

**Archaeology in the countryside**

3.22 For individual archaeological sites in the countryside, the provisions of PPG 16 are also important, especially those encouraging local authorities to require field evaluation of the character of sites and the likely impact of proposed development. The PPG's presumption against development which would adversely affect archaeology is highly relevant.

**Other features**

3.23 Other features which can be important in their contribution to the character and quality of the wider countryside, such as geological or landform features, historic parks and gardens, and battlefields, will often be designated in some way, and so will be covered by policies of the type described in Chapter 4. They are also likely to be incorporated in any policies relating to the conservation of landscape character or the historic landscape. However, where they are not, and where they are particularly important in a district, it could be appropriate to include a special policy for their protection. PPG 15 indicates (paragraphs 6.38 and 6.39) that planning authorities should protect parks and gardens included on English Heritage's *Register of parks and gardens of special historic interest* in preparing development plans and determining planning applications and should take account of the *Register of historic battlefields.* In both cases inclusion on the register is a material consideration in determining planning applications.

**The night sky**

3.24 Few would deny that the sky, and especially the night sky, is a special part of the experience of our surroundings. There is growing concern about the effects of outdoor lighting on the way that we see and enjoy starlit skies, twilight, and daybreak. There is a need to minimise light pollution of night skies and protect the remaining areas that are as yet unaffected, and planning policies can play an important role in this. Local plans should incorporate a suitable policy for development involving outside lighting.

**Box 3.6 Example policy on protection of field boundaries or other features important in the countryside**

Cotswold District Council includes the following policy in its 1994 proposed changes to the Deposit Draft Local Plan:

POLICY 42:

1 Where a development site contains or is bounded by Cotswold dry-stone or other walls, whatever their condition, every effort should be made to protect and repair them, as part of the development proposal. Where appropriate, the Council will impose a condition on any planning permission to ensure that this is done.

2 In locations where Cotswold dry-stone walls are characteristic, within Conservation Areas and the Cotswolds Areas of Outstanding Natural Beauty, new Cotswold dry-stone walls, of an appropriate type, height, and style, may be required for the boundaries and means of enclosure for new development, especially where boundaries are adjacent to highways, public footpaths or in prominent locations.

***Notes***

*The Council for the Protection of Rural England and the British Astronomical Association have produced a useful joint leaflet on the protection of the night sky, called* Starry, starry night. *It contains useful information, examples of District Plan policies on this topic, and other references.*

## Buildings and settlements in the countryside

3.25 Buildings and small settlements are an integral part of the countryside. Where they are of historic or vernacular character they can make a striking, and sometimes dominant, contribution to the character and quality of the landscape as well as having historic value in their own right. Some of the most important buildings and settlements will be protected by the special policies that apply to listed buildings and conservation areas (see Chapter 4). There is also, however, a need for plans to include policies which recognise the wider contribution of the more commonplace parts of the built environment which often generate the local character of an area (see PPG 15, paragraphs 6.1 and 6.2). The gradual erosion of such characteristics can often be as damaging as large-scale development.

3.26 We are particularly anxious to encourage careful consideration of:

- the building materials, building styles, and floorscape materials which are characteristic of different areas and settlements

- the form and pattern of characteristic hamlets and villages in the plan area, and the notable differences which may distinguish one type of settlement from another
- the harmony between buildings, open spaces, settlements, and the surrounding landscape
- the scale, height, density, and grouping of buildings in villages and, in particular, the importance of skylines, roofscapes, and landmark buildings such as churches when viewed from both inside and outside the settlement

These matters can best be described on the basis of an assessment of the character of the built environment, possibly through preparation of a Countryside Design Summary or a Conservation Area appraisal, or as a contribution to a landscape assessment. Such an

**Box 3.7 Example policy on the built environment and rural design in the countryside**

Cotswold District Council includes the following policy in its 1994 proposed changes to the Deposit Draft Local Plan:

POLICY 40:
All new development is expected to comply with the following Cotswold Design Code. Planning permission will not be given for development which fails to take proper account of that Code.

***Cotswold style***: a first class original modern design for a building will be preferable to a poor copy of a past style. Original modern designs should, however, reflect the existing distinctive Cotswold style, except in the newly created lakeside settings of the Cotswold Water Park, if they will not be seen in the context of an existing village, or where the scale or function of the building is such that the characteristics of the traditional Cotswold style cannot reasonably be applied. Newly created lakeside settings of the Cotswold Water Park also offer opportunities for different design solutions which are not in the Cotswold idiom, except where new buildings would be seen in the context of a village. In all such cases, buildings should still exhibit the highest standards of original modern architecture, and be in keeping with their surroundings.

***Setting***: the setting of any building should be carefully considered, whether in the countryside or in a built-up area. Attention should be paid to its impact on public views into, over, and out of the site. Those views should not be significantly harmed, and opportunities should be taken to enhance them or open up new views. In the countryside, or on the edge of towns and villages, buildings should be located to sit comfortably in the landscape. Buildings on the skyline should be avoided.

***Harmony and street scene***: new buildings should be in harmony with others around them. They can add interest and variety, but should not be out of keeping overall. They should be visually well-mannered towards their neighbours. Where buildings are arranged in gentle curves, irregular building lines, or sit on or close to the rear of the footpath, these local characteristics should be emulated in new development. New roofs should fit in with the roofscape of the area. Dormers which break up an unrelieved roof plane, where this is important to the character of a building, or rooflights which would spoil an unbroken vista of roofs, will not be permitted.

***Proportion***: new buildings should be well proportioned and relate to the human scale. All extensions should be in scale and character with the building to which they are added. Elevations should be in proportion with one another and with surrounding buildings. Excessive bulk should be avoided. The size, spacing, and location of openings should be in proportion and related to the function of the building and harmonious with its architectural style. Shop fronts should reflect the character and architectural style of the upper floors, the distinction between separate buildings, be of materials and colours appropriate to the building, and be well proportioned in themselves.

***Simplicity, detail, and decoration***: as a general principle, the design of new buildings should be simple, avoiding over-fussy detailing. Within this principle, opportunities should be taken to add interesting details, ornamentation, and expressions of local craftsmanship. The nature and colour of external woodwork, cladding, and rainwater goods, should harmonise or successfully contrast with the colour of the walling materials. Large new buildings on the edge of towns or villages or in the open countryside should be finished or clad in subdued, usually dark, colours.

***Materials***: new buildings should be constructed of materials typical of, and used in similar proportions to, those traditionally used in the immediate surroundings. Special care should be taken in the AONB, Special Landscape Areas, and Conservation Areas, and for development which affects the appearance, character or setting of a listed building, where natural Cotswold stone, other traditional Cotswold materials and finishes, or very high quality modern substitutes only should be used.

***Craftsmanship***: building materials, particularly Cotswold stone, should be used in the traditional manner, with careful attention to its bedding or 'grain', the width of courses, the colour and type of pointing, the diminishing courses of stone slates, and the texture and materials used in rendered finishes. The Council will normally require the construction of sample panels on-site, to be approved before building work commences, and to be kept for reference throughout the work.

assessment should address building materials, traditional architecture, settlement patterns, the economic base of the area, and the way that the built environment has evolved.

3.27 All new development in the countryside needs to take account of these considerations if character and 'sense of place' are to be retained. In practice this means, as far as possible, keeping buildings of historic or vernacular character, however unassuming, in a state of good repair and in positive, appropriate use. It also means giving attention to securing appropriate complementary design for new development. Particular care needs to be taken over the siting and design of affordable housing in the countryside when this takes place outside the existing village envelopes.

3.28 Some plans already include policies to encourage design of new development that is appropriate to the locality, and some are including reference to design codes as part of these policies. We welcome the inclusion of such policies and wish to encourage all District Plans to give attention to these matters for rural areas. However, we think that detailed advice on rural design should be dealt with in supplementary planning guidance rather than in the main body of plans where it would lead to excessive detail.

3.29 Policies on rural design, and the justifications which support them, should clearly indicate the materials, building types and styles, settlement forms, and building groupings which are especially important to the character of the countryside, if necessary distinguishing between different areas. Landscape assessment can often help with this by identifying a range of different types of landscape and describing the contribution which buildings and settlements make to their character. Conservation area appraisal techniques are also relevant. Policies should also indicate how these characteristics should be taken into account in proposals for new development. The aim should be to encourage proposals which reinforce or enhance the special sense of place created by the built environment in the countryside and to discourage those which undermine it.

3.30 Where local traditional materials are particularly important, sources of supply may be a problem and reuse of salvaged materials has been seen as a way of maintaining local character. However, the supply of such materials is finite and over-use can result in the demolition of buildings which in themselves contribute to local character. In some cases the reopening of traditional sources of supply may be more appropriate and local authorities should consider including policies to allow this.

***Notes***

*The question of rural design is dealt with in Annex A of PPG 1 which states (paragraph A1) that the appearance of proposed development and its relationship to its surroundings are material considerations. It goes on to say (paragraph A6) that development plans should provide applicants with clear indications of the planning authorities' design expectations, but should avoid excessive prescription and detail. Design is also referred to in PPGs 7 and 12.*

*The Countryside Commission has carried out research on the topic of buildings and design in the countryside and published its findings in* Design in the countryside *(CCP 418, 1993) and* Design in the countryside experiments *(CCP 473, 1994) as part of a continuing programme.*

*Although emphasis on local traditional materials is important it should be noted that, because of Article 30 of the Treaty of Rome, use of equivalent natural materials that are not local cannot be ruled out.*

**Box 3.8 Example policy on enhancement in the countryside**

Hambleton District Council includes the following policy in its 1994 Draft, District-wide Local Plan:

POLICY L11:
Special emphasis will be placed on the creation of new landscapes and the general visual improvement of the landscape in the areas shown as Landscape Enhancement Areas on the proposals map and inset maps. Within these areas, landscape creation, improvement, and enhancement will be secured and promoted by:

- encouraging, and where necessary, requiring new development permitted by other policies to incorporate major on- and off-site landscaping. When considering larger-scale developments their potential to enhance the visual quality of the landscape will be taken into account
- encouraging the conservation and maintenance of features important to the local landscape such as trees, hedges, copses, woodlands, and ponds
- encouraging the removal of eyesores and redundant structures
- encouraging the planting of trees, copses, and woodlands in large blocks in accord with policy L13
- encouraging landscape work to reduce the impact of existing intrusive development

## Enhancement in the countryside

3.31 There are often many opportunities to enhance the rural environment where degradation has resulted in loss of character and quality. The causes of such degradation are many and varied and include inappropriate or poorly designed development, mineral extraction followed by inadequate or inappropriate restoration, waste disposal, industrial dereliction, neglect or abandonment of land, and agricultural intensification.

3.32 In such circumstances proposals for enhancement can do a great deal to create new landscapes or new habitats for wildlife, to improve the surroundings of historic features or to repair the historic fabric of the landscape. Local plans deal only with the development and land use aspects of enhancement, but the supporting justifications can provide more information about the opportunities, the constraints, and the ways of achieving enhancement.

3.33 Potential for securing enhancement should not provide a reason for departing from otherwise restrictive policies towards development. Nor should it be allowed to encourage neglect of historic buildings or degradation of land and so be used as a lever to secure permission for development. With this proviso policies and proposals in plans should ensure that:

- essential and appropriate new development contributes wherever possible to enhancing degraded environments

- proposals for enhancement, including those linked to new development, do not unwittingly cause damage to conservation interests: for example, derelict industrial land may have both nature conservation and industrial archaeological value, and more locally small patches of apparently waste ground may be highly valued by local people for dog walking or children's play.

3.34 New development can contribute to enhancement in a number of ways. For example, it may be possible to:

- remove structural eyesores or other intrusive features

- restore existing landscape features in the area and create new ones by appropriate landscaping proposals

- create new wildlife habitats

- expose geological features of interest

- enhance the setting of archaeological or historic features

- create new access opportunities, such as paths, meadows or picnic areas which help to meet local needs

Policies may indicate where, and under what circumstances, such enhancement may be appropriate. It is probable that Section 106 agreements, as discussed in Chapter 2, may be the appropriate mechanism for achieving this.

3.35 Where provision for such enhancement is included in plans, reference needs to be made to ways of securing appropriate management for any new features or habitats that may be created, especially if they are part of a development proposal. Ensuring appropriate long-term management is critical if the money initially spent on enhancement is not to be wasted.

## Specific types of environment

3.36 Certain environments will derive special benefit from a coordinated approach in terms of development control and environmental management and enhancement. The most obvious examples of these are the coast and river environments, but the principle of integration may be equally applicable in other environments. Such areas cross administrative boundaries. In these circumstances, non-statutory strategies or management plans specific to an obvious geographical unit (eg a river valley, river catchment or coastal unit) have an important role to play, particularly where they are recognised by all the constituent local authorities. Land use policies contained in such strategies can then be incorporated into the statutory development plans of the participating local authorities to ensure cross-boundary continuity of approach.

**The coast and marine environment**

3.37 We are particularly anxious to conserve and enhance the distinctive character of coastal areas, of which 75% in England remain undeveloped. They embrace some of our most important and cherished landscapes and are of considerable ecological value. They have a wealth of valuable archaeological, historical, and cultural features, including those in the intertidal zone, especially where archaeological landscapes have been inundated and in areas of historic coastal defences. They are also highly complex systems, especially in terms of the physical processes of erosion and deposition which shape them, in turn resulting in many geomorphological features of value and interest.

3.38 They face many pressures, including investigations into tidal barrages, major marina developments, and on-shore transfer, processing, and storage of off-shore drilling for oil and gas. In addition, global warming and rising sea levels necessitate a decision on the limits which

**Box 3.9 Example policy on coastal areas**

East Lindsey District Council includes the following policy in its 1994 proposed amendments to the Deposit Local Plan:

C17:
Within CCA1 and CCA4 development will not be permitted unless it is essential in that location. In particular, no built development shall be permitted on or to the seaward side of the sandhills. Where permitted, development shall not materially harm the amenities, character or ecological balance of the area because of its siting, scale, form, appearance, materials, noise or fume emissions, or traffic generation.

should be placed on coastal development in areas liable to flooding and coastal erosion.

3.39 There is a need for integrated planning of the coast, with full recognition of its conservation values. PPG 20 encourages cooperative working in the preparation of development plans between local authorities around estuaries and along stretches of the open coast. Wherever possible we suggest that natural coastal units (or cells), which recognise the scale over which natural coastal processes operate, should be used as the basis for coastal management, planning, and enhancement.

3.40 Our particular concerns are that:

- undeveloped coastline should be retained

- emphasis is placed on working with, rather than against, natural processes when protecting development from flooding and coastal erosion, including giving consideration to the managed retreat of sea defences, with its potential benefits for conservation (PPG 20 paragraph 2.19), provided that it does not have an adverse effect on archaeological deposits or on any other elements of the historic environment

- coastal development is limited to that for which a coastal location is essential (PPG 20, paragraphs 2.9 and 2.10)

- any new development does not, for the foreseeable future, exacerbate existing problems of coastal protection or result in altered patterns of erosion, deposition or flooding elsewhere along the coast to the detriment of important habitats or coastal features

- very careful consideration is given to the direct and indirect implications of land reclamation on conservation interests

- areas of open coastline, including estuaries, are protected from isolated development

- where new development is acceptable in principle, it is judged in terms of its implications for both land and sea, including views from the sea, marine pollution, effects on marine wildlife, etc

- a zonal policy is pursued for coastal recreation, concentrating active recreation in existing built-up areas and including remote zones where the emphasis is on nature conservation and appropriate low-key access

3.41 A range of different policies within a local plan may have a direct bearing on coastal areas. Substantial lengths of coast are of national or international importance for landscape, nature conservation or for cultural or historic importance and reference should therefore be made, as appropriate, to landscape policies (National Parks, AONBs, Heritage Coasts), to nature conservation policies ( SACs, SPAs, Ramsar sites, MNRs, NNRs, and SSSIs), and policies concerning the conservation of archaeological and cultural features of interest (see Chapter 4 for details). Other relevant policy areas may include those concerned with environmental enhancement, energy provision, including that from renewable sources, for example tidal barrages and wind, countryside access, major coastal tourism developments including marinas, and mineral exploitation.

***Notes***

*All issues relating to flooding and coastal protection will need to be discussed in detail with the NRA.*

*The Department of the Environment supports the voluntary preparation of Coastal Management Plans by groups of organisations working together, as described in the document* Managing the coast *(1993). Such plans provide a structure within which local authorities and others can take positive action to assist in the implementation of planning objectives and policies. Other useful material can be found in* Conserving England's marine heritage - a strategy *(English Nature 1993).*

*MAFF, together with the National Rivers Authority and others responsible for coastal defences, is also involved in the preparation of Shoreline Management Plans to address key areas of coastal policy and provide a framework for sustainable coastal defence strategies.*

*Estuaries are often under particularly severe pressure and wherever possible development should be guided by an Estuary Management Plan drawn up by all interested parties, including the relevant local authorities, and aimed at securing the sustainable management of the estuary. Useful references include* A strategy for the sustainable use of England's estuaries *(English Nature 1993);* Estuary management plans - a co-ordinator's guide *(English Nature 1993) and* Conserving England's marine heritage - a strategy *(English Nature 1993).*

**River corridors and catchments**

3.42 Rivers and river valleys likewise have distinctive landscapes, are highly valued for recreation, and are often of great wildlife interest including a range of increasingly uncommon water-dependent habitats of the floodplain. They are also associated with rich assemblages of archaeological, historical, and cultural features. They can, however, be a focus of conflict, for example with continuing development in the floodplain necessitating flood alleviation works which are out of sympathy with the river's natural character or gravel extraction leading to the loss of valuable archaeological remains associated with river terraces.

3.43 As a result, river corridors (ie areas of land physically and visually linked to a river) may need special policies to minimise the conflict between conservation and development and to manage and enhance their valuable linear character. In some cases it may be appropriate to provide policies for the larger natural unit of the river catchment, working alongside

**Box 3.10 Example policy on river corridors/river catchments**

East Lindsey District Council includes the following policy in its 1994 Deposit Local Plan:

ENV17:
Development will be permitted where it can be shown that it will not harm the open character, nature conservation importance or recreational importance of the river corridors of the rivers Witham, Steeping, Bain, Lud, Waring and Lym, and of the Louth Navigation Canal, Great Eau and Grift Drains.

the NRA's initiative of developing catchment management plans which consider the complex interactions between the water environment and the land uses of the whole catchment. Local authorities should ensure that their detailed policies or proposals do not compromise those of neighbouring authorities in the same river catchment.

3.44 In particular we would wish to see emphasis placed on:

- the retention of river washlands through the careful control of land raising and any new built development in river floodplains, thereby reducing the necessity for more and potentially intrusive and damaging flood alleviation works
- the careful assessment of the direct and indirect effects of new development on the river regime, including the effects of surface run-off on flood flows and water table levels, especially where flood or water-dependent habitats are involved
- avoiding direct and indirect damage to archaeological remains within the river corridor, especially those which are dependent on the retention of specific water table conditions
- the promotion of river corridors as important areas of open land both within and across local authority boundaries, with special emphasis placed on their value as wildlife and amenity corridors, especially within and on the edge of urban areas
- the need for design of new developments adjacent to rivers to reflect their riverine setting and avoidance of culverting of river lengths
- the restoration to a more natural character of downgraded or highly engineered sections of river channel, including reestablishing continuity with adjacent water-dependent floodplain habitats

***Notes***
*Other policies within a local plan which may be of particular relevance to river corridors and catchments include those relating to the conservation of key landscapes (eg AONBs), important habitats (eg SACs, SPAs, Ramsar sites, SSSIs, LNRs, and sites of regional and local significance for nature conservation), and sites of archaeological and cultural significance, and policies concerned with environmental enhancement, wildlife corridors, protection of water resources, public access, mineral extraction, and waste disposal.*

*Useful information is produced in the National Rivers Authority document* Guidance notes for local planning authorities on the methods of protecting the water environment through development plans *(1994).*

## The urban environment

3.45 In some respects the division between town and country is an artificial one, and most of the principles outlined above are also applicable to urban environments, but there are also many specific considerations which apply to towns and cities. Here, as in the countryside, it is equally important to give attention to the environment as a whole and not just to the special, designated areas. People in towns and cities have a special need for contact with nature, and urban green space and the character and quality of the built environment are increasingly recognised as contributing significantly to the quality of urban life and to the economy. We need towns and cities where people can enjoy living and where the environment encourages involvement, understanding, and education. These are important objectives in their own right, but can also help to reduce the desire of people to move out from the cities and help to reduce development pressure in rural areas, attract development, and maintain a healthy economy.

3.46 We therefore believe that it is important to maintain and enhance the character and quality of the built environment in towns and cities, to take full account of the need to protect features of archaeological or historical interest, to protect and manage open space, to conserve areas of 'countryside' and green corridors that survive within the urban fabric, and to allow urban wildlife to thrive.

**Box 3.11 Local plan checklist for the urban environment**

We expect plans with urban areas to include policies to:

- maintain, conserve, and enhance all the various elements of the historic built environment
- protect archaeology in the urban environment
- protect and enhance important open land, including areas of importance for nature conservation
- protect the countryside around towns and cities

**Box 3.12 Example policy on conserving and enhancing the built environment in towns**

Guildford Borough Council included the following policy in its 1993 Local Plan:

36BE:
In considering development proposals in conservation areas, the Council will not normally be prepared to consider outline planning applications. All proposals for new development should preserve or enhance the character or appearance of the area and give consideration to the following:

- the retention of buildings, groups of buildings, existing street patterns, building lines, and ground surfaces, and the impact on significant open spaces
- the retention of architectural features such as walls and shop fronts and other features which contribute to the character of the area
- the impact of the development on the townscape and roofscape of the conservation area and the need to apply a consistently high standard of design
- the need to ensure the protection of trees which contribute to the character and appearance of the conservation area
- the need or scope to remove unsightly and inappropriate features or details

**The historic built environment**

3.47 Towns, like the countryside around them, have evolved over the centuries to reach their present form. They are all therefore historic to some degree, and though many of the most important historic areas and buildings will usually have been designated as conservation areas or listed buildings, much of the remainder will also make an important contribution to the character of urban areas and their rural hinterland.

3.48 As with rural areas, assessment of character is the key to developing sensitive policies and proposals. This requires careful assessment, firstly of the relationship of a town to its physical setting in the landscape, of the way that it has evolved in response to this as well as to social, economic or political influences, and of its archaeology. The origin and age of different areas needs to be established, the urban morphology understood, and areas or features of historic or architectural interest identified. Characteristic building materials, styles, and local traditions must be investigated, as must urban form and townscape. The historic form of the town, including its burgage plots, open spaces, parks and garden areas, its defences or street patterns, and the way that these relate to the built fabric, will be particularly important in establishing urban character. The location of key landmark buildings, the nature of views to them, important landscape features, and important approaches to the town will all need to be documented. Techniques such as formal 'plan analysis' (the characterisation of historic zones dating from different periods of a town's history) may be helpful.

3.49 Policies should ensure that, as far as possible, new development takes account of the character and quality of the built environment and the way in which a town has grown and evolved. When development proposals affect the periphery of the town, the relationship with the surrounding countryside and suburban areas will be particularly important. Here containment, by Green Belt or similar tools, will be the focus of policies.

3.50 Other issues that need to be taken into account in formulating policies are:

- effects of proposals for peripheral development including the effects of commercial schemes on the economy and fabric of the town centre and on urban form
- effects of residential development in generating additional pressure for services and transport
- effects of town centre development pressures
- nature and extent of advertisements and their effect on the character of the town
- character and quality of public spaces and spaces between buildings
- design of shop fronts and signing in relation to character
- appropriate treatment of land which is in the public domain
- effects on the vitality and the physical fabric of towns of under-use of upper floors
- pressures to convert residential accommodation to office and other commercial uses
- constraints of below-ground archaeological deposits on buildings

Some of these issues are considered further in Chapters 6 and 7.

3.51 All these considerations need to be reflected in devising land use allocations, development policies, and guidance on design. Policies on design will have an important role to play in encouraging development which is sympathetic to the historic character and quality of towns. It should also be possible to identify degraded or derelict areas, or areas suffering the effects of incongruous development, where redevelopment may help to achieve enhancement.

**Archaeology in the urban environment**

3.52 Historic towns and cities, especially those which have occupied their sites since the Roman period, provide some of the largest and archaeologically most complex sites in the country. The buried archaeological deposits accumulated from continuous occupation over the centuries are extremely important in their own right, as well as being part of the wider historic urban environment. Many extensive archaeological excavations over the last fifty years have added to our knowledge of the urban archaeological resource and provided guidance on the need for sound strategies for future management. Much of this resource is unprotected and is highly vulnerable, for example to operations such as trench digging by statutory undertakers.

3.53 Some of the more clearly defined monuments of archaeological or historical importance in a national context in urban areas will be scheduled as ancient monuments under Part I of the Ancient Monuments and Archaeological Areas Act 1979. Others will fall within Conservation Areas. These special cases are considered further in Chapter 4. In general, however, archaeology in towns relies on the planning system for protection or recording.

3.54 PPG 16 is especially relevant for planning authorities who have important archaeological resources in their towns or cities. The provisions relating to desk-based and field assessments are particularly important, since they place the responsibility on the developer to assess the potential impacts of their proposals when early discussions with the local authority indicate that an area where important remains may exist might be affected. Local plans clearly have a role in flagging such areas, but even where there is no prior discussion, the PPG stresses that applications still need to be properly assessed for their potential archaeological effects and places the onus on developers to ensure that this assessment takes place.

3.55 Managing the urban archaeological resource is an important and complex matter. The resource is very important and the pressures for change highly significant, so the task of management is extremely challenging. Local authorities must have proper frameworks in place for protecting and managing urban archaeology, making use of the appropriate legislation and planning guidance. They must also have access to archaeological databases or strategies of the type sponsored by English Heritage.

3.56 Such databases will inform a strategic assessment of a town's archaeology which will probably provide the best way of integrating archaeology into the planning process in urban areas in the future. This will allow for increasingly informed planning policies and development control decisions. It will also provide the basis for assessments of current knowledge and understanding of the archaeology of historic towns, including the definition of future research strategies, as well as for urban strategies to protect and manage them.

3.57 Local plans should therefore recognise the importance of the urban archaeological resource, and acknowledge that it comprises both known and

**Box 3.13 Example policy on urban archaeology**

The City of Westminster includes the following policy in its 1995 proposed modifications to the deposit draft of the Unitary Development Plan:

DES18:
(A) The City Council will promote the conservation, protection, and enhancement of the archaeological heritage of Westminster and its interpretation and presentation to the public. Where development may affect land of known or potential archaeological importance, the city council will expect applicants to properly assess and plan for the archaeological implications of their proposals. The policies in (B) and (C) below may apply elsewhere where the archaeological evidence suggests that this would be appropriate.

(B) Within the City Council's Areas of Special Archaeological Priority a written assessment of the likely archaeological impact of development (archaeological statement) will normally be required as part of the documentation needed to complete a planning application whenever it is proposed to carry out any excavations or other ground works.

(C) With the Area of Special Archaeological Priority the City Council may request, where necessary information cannot be supplied by other means, that an on-site assessment by trial work (archaeological field evaluation) is carried out before any decision on the planning application is taken.

(D) The City Council will seek to ensure that nationally important archaeological remains and their settings are permanently preserved *in situ* and where appropriate are given statutory protection. In such cases, if preservation *in situ* is both desirable and feasible, the city council will require the development design to accommodate this objective.

(E) Where the preservation of archaeological remains *in situ* is not appropriate, the City Council will require that no development takes place on a site until archaeological investigations have been carried out by a reputable investigating body. Such investigations shall be in accordance with a detailed scheme to be approved in advance by the City Council.

**Box 3.14 Example policy on open spaces and urban areas**

East Lindsey District Council includes the following policy in its 1994 proposed changes to the Deposit Local Plan:

ENV20:
Development will be permitted on open spaces and frontages, which are identified on the inset maps as being protected, provided significant harm will not be caused to their appearance, character or the role they play in meeting one or more of the criteria set out below:

- preventing the coalescence of settlements
- providing the settings for listed or important historical buildings, scheduled archaeological monuments or other amenity features
- providing an important visual element in the street scene
- framing or enabling an important view to exist
- providing a buffer between non-complementary uses
- comprising or providing important historic or geological features
- providing the settings for well defined demarcation between the edge of a settlement and the countryside
- providing well defined visual relief in an otherwise built-up frontage, particularly in the case of ribbon development extending into the countryside

As well as the identified sites, there may be other sites which also meet one or more of the above criteria but which have not yet been included. In the event of a development proposal being made on such a site, the Council will consider whether it should be afforded the same level of protection.

documented areas as well as poorly understood zones, individual features, both buried and visible, and factors which influence the modern townscape, such as street grids, patterns of property tenure, and groups of buildings. Policies should clearly demonstrate that the provisions of PPG 16 will apply and indicate the primacy of preservation *in situ* of significant deposits, and should provide a framework for the assessment of the proposed impacts of development in those areas where insufficient information exists. Supporting text should describe the relationships between local plan policy, its associated archaeological strategy, and the information base upon which the strategy and policy are based.

**Protecting and enhancing open land in towns and cities**

3.58 Within urban areas there is a wide range of open spaces of different types, fulfilling many different functions. They include, among others, private gardens, public parks and gardens, informal parks, playing fields, allotments, small enclaves of remnant farmland, urban woodland, cemeteries, areas of derelict or disused land, and river and stream corridors. Many of these open spaces are invaluable in providing landscape features, wildlife habitat, accessible open space, and play areas. They can be particularly important in creating 'green chains' to provide links and stepping stones for wildlife. Many, notably the surroundings of ancient monuments such as castles, abbeys or monasteries, parks, and cemeteries, may be of historic or archaeological interest, perhaps as designed landscapes, or may be of archaeological importance. Government guidance on open space is set out in PPG 17, *Sport and recreation*, particularly in paragraphs 3 and 4.

3.59 Policies and proposals should protect existing areas of green space which are considered to be important for landscape or local amenity, for access and enjoyment, as wildlife habitat, in providing stepping stones or corridors of value for the movement of wildlife or for their historical or archaeological value. Proposals for development which are acceptable should, wherever possible, include provision for the appropriate enhancement of adjoining open areas, taking full account of their existing interest. The spaces are often of special value to local people who need to be closely involved in planning for their future. Where there is a shortage of such vital urban open space (which can be defined as 'areas of green space deficiency') policies should be designed to rectify this, in some cases by provisions related to new development.

***Notes***

*The most important open areas may already have some form of designation, for example as Sites of Special Scientific Interest, but the important thing is to recognise the value of all sorts of open space throughout the urban area, not just the special, designated areas.*

*Open spaces of townscape significance will increasingly be referred to in conservation area appraisals as features which contribute positively to the character of these areas.*

## The countryside around towns and cities

3.60 The relationship of towns to the surrounding countryside is often critical to their character. It is the open countryside which, if properly protected, sets finite limits to the growth of a town, defining the character of the all-important urban edge and maintaining the focus of the urban area. Open land which extends into the town is also extremely important, often bringing corridors of countryside right into large built-up areas and providing links for the movement of wildlife between town and country. In addition to its strategic role in relation to the developed area the open land around towns may be important for landscape and wildlife, and in some cases may have historic significance. It also offers an important resource for access and enjoyment which can be reached easily without the need for long journeys by car, and can provide important opportunities for educational use.

3.61 Proximity to large populations means, however, that in these areas there are exceptional pressures for new development, and farming may be difficult. As a result, the landscape fabric can easily become neglected and degraded and in consequence 'the urban fringe' is frequently viewed in a negative light. Containment of the spread of the urban area and protection of these open areas in and around towns from inappropriate development is therefore important, as is the need for positive management of these areas.

**Green Belts**

3.62 Green Belts are a long-standing strategic planning tool designed primarily to control the spread of development and the coalescence of towns. Among other acknowledged achievements Green Belts afford protection to the countryside around most of England's major urban areas. The 1995 revision of PPG 2 reaffirms, with minor modifications, the traditional purposes of defining Green Belts and emphasises that their fundamental aim is to keep land permanently open. These purposes include checking urban sprawl, preventing coalescence of adjacent towns, safeguarding the countryside from encroachment, preserving the setting and special character of historic towns, and assisting in urban regeneration.

3.63 Although Green Belts are not defined on the basis of landscape character or other environmental criteria, PPG 2 now for the first time sets out a set of positive objectives for the use of land in defined Green Belts. They are:

- to provide opportunities for access to the open countryside for the urban population
- to provide opportunities for outdoor sport and outdoor recreation near urban areas
- to retain attractive landscapes, and enhance landscapes, near to where people live
- to improve damaged and derelict land around towns
- to secure nature conservation interest
- to retain land in agricultural, forestry, and related uses

3.64 We welcome this and wish to encourage local authorities to reflect such positive objectives in development plan policies. Green Belt policies should state clearly the requirement for restraint on inappropriate development and make a commitment to pursuing the positive objectives for Green Belts as listed in PPG 2. In terms of our interests they should emphasise:

- the need to conserve and enhance the character and quality of the landscape and features of nature conservation value or of archaeological, historical or cultural significance
- provision of opportunities for access and enjoyment which minimise the need to travel further afield for recreation, and encourage use of public transport linked to 'green' modes of travel like cycling and walking

**Box 3.15 Example policy dealing with use of the Green Belts**

Broxtowe Borough Council includes the following policy in its 1994 Local Plan:

EV4:
Within the context set by policy EV1, the Borough Council will encourage use of Green Belt land which increases the potential for public access, recreation, tourism and landscape improvement.

***Notes***

*PPG 2 also maintains the presumption against inappropriate development within Green Belts and refines the categories of appropriate development. Its policies on reuse of buildings, including farm buildings, are designed to be more in line with policies for the wider countryside. This issue is discussed in Chapter 8. They include, however, additional safeguards to preserve the openness of Green Belt land.*

*Recent studies have shown that there can be significant change in the environment of Green Belts in part as a result of types of development considered to be appropriate. Outdoor sport can pose particular problems, especially where it involves substantial building, car parks or floodlighting, or other development which can harm the character of the environment. In accordance with PPG 2, policies should indicate that only facilities which 'are genuinely required for uses of land which preserve the openness of the Green Belt and do not conflict with the purposes of including land in it' should be permitted.*

*A research study, involving English Heritage, the Department of the Environment, Cheshire County Council, and Chester City Council, has examined a number of relevant issues with special reference to Chester, a historic town surrounded by a Green Belt, with many pressures for development. Details are in the study report* Environmental capacity: a methodology for historic cities *(Chester City Council 1995).*

**Other open land**

3.65 Where there is no Green Belt, important areas of open land which separate settlements, provide important gaps of open countryside or penetrate into towns and cities, could, where appropriate, be identified as 'green wedges', 'countryside gaps' or 'green corridors'. Policies to protect these areas and the supporting justifications need to draw attention to the value of these areas for landscape and amenity, wildlife, historic significance, and access and enjoyment, as well as restricting development, and to indicate the importance of appropriate management of such land.

**Box 3.16 Example policy on protecting open land as green wedges or green corridors**

Hambleton District Council includes the following policy in its 1994 Deposit Draft, District-wide Local Plan.

G4:
The following green wedges as shown on the inset maps, will be protected and enhanced...Within these areas development will not normally be permitted where it would adversely affect their open character, visual amenity, recreation and wildlife value or compromise the gap between settlements. Development within or adjacent to green wedges will be discouraged or, where necessary, required to make a positive contribution to them.

## Positive approaches to the urban fringe

3.66 The emphasis on sustainable development means that there is now an urgent need for a more comprehensive approach to the planning of the urban fringe, recognising that it is the most accessible countryside to the majority of the population. It offers wide-ranging opportunities for recreation, potentially reached by integrated public transport linked to 'green' modes of travel, such as walking and cycling. It also offers opportunities for recycling derelict and downgraded land for redevelopment, linked with wider initiatives for environmental enhancement. The Community Forest initiative (dealt with in paragraphs 3.68-9 below) provides an example of such a comprehensive approach to strategic planning in the urban fringe.

3.67 Our particular concerns in the urban fringe are:

- to seek a positive approach to the conservation and enhancement of these areas, with special emphasis placed on maintaining and restoring local character and sense of place

- to promote the value of these areas for quiet enjoyment of the countryside and to ensure appropriate management of countryside recreation

- to control new development, with special emphasis on protecting the scale, setting, form, and structure of historic towns, recognising that they have a finite limit to growth

- to recognise the opportunities that development may offer to enhance degraded urban fringe landscapes, provided that the existing interest of such land, either for wildlife or industrial archaeology, is safeguarded

- to seek proper management and enhancement of these often pressured landscapes

***Notes***
*Other policies in local plans which may be of direct relevance include those concerned with the maintenance and enhancement of the rural environment, the conservation of habitats including the designation of Local Nature Reserves, the maintenance and enhancement of historic towns, the promotion of countryside access, public transport and integrated transport strategies, minerals and waste disposal, and active recreation and sport with particular reference to golf courses, noisy sports, and horse riding.*

*The Countryside Commission's programme of Countryside Management is a well established method of promoting countryside access and achieving management and enhancement of the urban fringe.*

**Community Forests**
3.68 The Community Forest Programme is a joint initiative between the Countryside Commission, the Forestry Commission, and the relevant local authorities to promote the creation, regeneration, and multi-purpose use of well wooded landscapes around major towns and cities. Each Community Forest has a non-statutory Forest Plan, prepared with public consultation, which is then submitted to the Government for approval. The Countryside Commission and the Forestry Commission, in partnership with the relevant local authorities, have appointed a locally based project team in each Community Forest. Neither the existence of a Community Forest nor the approval of a Forest Plan changes the statutory planning framework for an area. The role and responsibilities of the local planning authority are unaffected, and the local Community Forest teams do not have any statutory role within the land use planning system.

3.69 Policies and proposals which are likely to provide the basis for deciding planning applications or determining conditions to be attached to planning permissions should be set out in the development plan, which is subject to statutory procedures. It is therefore important that Community Forest objectives should be fully reflected in appropriate policies within the development plan. Local plans should address agreed Community Forests by:

- showing the Community Forest boundary on the proposal map

- providing, in the reasoned justification, a brief description of the nature and benefits of the Community Forest and the intentions for implementation, cross-referring to the Forest Plan for further background

**Box 3.17 Example policy on the countryside around towns**

Chelmsford Borough Council includes the following policy in its 1993 Deposit Draft Local Plan:

RE17:
Any development in the urban fringe must include proposals for protecting existing features and for the positive enhancement of the landscape. Proposals for woodland planting in appropriate locations would normally be supported.

- including development control policies which facilitate the establishment of agreed Community Forests and provide that any development proposals within them should respect the woodland setting. Such policies might include:
  - support for appropriate small-scale development which is integral to the Community Forest
  - provision to assess the potential for an appropriate positive contribution to the Community Forest from any significant development taking place within its area
  - guidance on the circumstances in which it may be necessary to negotiate planning obligations to enable development to go ahead. Such obligations may, in certain circumstances, include off-site works provided there is a clear relationship between such works and the development itself. Advice on the use of planning obligations is contained in DOE Circular 16/91.
  - cross-referencing to other relevant policies in the plan, including nature conservation, archaeology, agriculture, water protection, economy, and leisure and recreation
  - referring to any Supplementary Planning Guidance derived from the Forest Plan
  - coordinating similar policies for all local plans across one Community Forest
  - including references to the preparation of development briefs for specific sites where appropriate

Local plans should make it clear that planning permission for inappropriate developments will not be granted simply because applicants are prepared to plant trees or otherwise assist the Forest Plan. Similarly, permission for otherwise acceptable development should not be refused simply because a developer is unwilling to plant trees or provide a financial contribution to assist Community Forest objectives.

3.70 A number of Community Forest areas overlap wholly or partially with Green Belts. Community Forests provide an effective mechanism for achieving the positive objectives for the use of land in Green Belts as set out in PPG 2. In respect of development proposals which lie within Green Belt areas of Community Forests, local plans should apply the policies advocated in paragraph 3.69 above, in so far as they are compatible with the provisions of PPG 2 and the normal policies controlling development in Green Belts.

# Chapter 4 Conserving key environmental resources

## Introduction

4.1 Chapter 3 has described our approach to the conservation of the wider environment. The conservation of key environmental resources (the 'critical environment capital') is also at the heart of our approach to sustainable development (as outlined in Chapter 2). These resources are now considered here, separately from our more general concern for the wider environment, in all its diversity. This chapter concentrates on the environmental resources which are identified as being special or 'critical', either at the international or national level, or more locally.

4.2 Definitions of environmental resources are still evolving, and there is widespread debate about how they relate to environmental capacity. Not all our 'critical' environmental resources can be considered as completely static and unchanging. They must continue to be used and managed in appropriate ways which respect their value, but equally must be given rigorous protection from inappropriate and damaging change from development or new land uses.

4.3 Our aim is to encourage local authorities to devise policies which give an appropriate level of protection to key environmental resources, according to their level of importance. Resources which are internationally or nationally important must be given the strongest protection because they are part of our national, or indeed global, environmental heritage. Other resources which are important at the regional, county or more local level also merit protection, but there is a need for a clear distinction between policies for these areas and those for the primary national designations. In effect this means developing a hierarchy of policies. The Secretary of State for the Environment, in a statement made in 1993, urged planning authorities to be cautious about introducing local designations because they may place unnecessary barriers in the way of economic activity. The statement also recognised, however, that such designations may be appropriate where there is reason to believe that the normal planning policies cannot be applied to provide the necessary protection.

4.4 In dealing with the protection of key environmental resources our different interests may sometimes need to be individually addressed. The specific requirements of landscape conservation and enhancement, nature conservation, and archaeological and building conservation need to be clearly articulated in carefully worded policies, though the links between them should also be indicated where relevant.

4.5 Many of these key environmental resources are cultural rather than natural, even in the case of wildlife habitats. As the Government's UK Biodiversity Action Plan states:

> although geology, geomorphology, soils and climate have set the limits for biological diversity in the UK, people have now become the prime regulators for the biodiversity we see around us. Much of the land surface is now farmed, forested, lived in or worked upon: even our most remote hills and mountain tops are grazed or trampled.

4.6 This means that they cannot be expected to remain completely unchanged, because there will be some evolution in response to continuing land use and management. That is why there is growing emphasis on the assessment and characterisation of these special areas (for example, on landscape assessment of AONBs, character analysis of conservation areas, and descriptions of the special interest of SSSIs). Such characterisations and descriptions are designed to specify what it is about the site or area that is special, as a basis for carefully tailored policies to protect their value.

4.7 Because these environmental resources are of such importance, we wish to ensure that local plans contain appropriate policies to ensure that development or land use change which could adversely affect their special character and qualities is not permitted. The wording of such policies is important.

4.8 Our view is that for our most important nationally designated areas the phrasing should indicate that inappropriate development which would have significant adverse effects, either directly or indirectly, on the special character, quality or interest of the area will not be permitted. This would place the onus on the developer to demonstrate that any proposal would not have such effects. In some cases, especially in the case of important nature conservation or historical sites, but also for major development in National Parks and AONBs, it may be necessary to indicate very exceptional circumstances where development may be permitted. For internationally or nationally important sites these circumstances could be defined as a proven public interest which overrides the value of the resource, where the need cannot be met in another less damaging location. Policies for other environmental resources, important at the regional, county or more local level, should be more flexible, while still seeking to protect the character and value of such areas by establishing clear criteria against which development proposals would be judged.

4.9 In dealing with key environmental resources we wish to ensure that local plans give proper attention to conserving and enhancing:

- important landscapes, valued for their scenic or historic character

• important sites, areas or species of nature conservation importance

• important archaeological resources and components of the historic built environment

## Important landscapes

4.10 Substantial parts of the English countryside have been designated as being of national importance, either as National Parks and equivalent areas, Areas of Outstanding Natural Beauty or Heritage Coasts. A few landscape areas have been given international status as World Heritage Sites. Counties and districts also frequently identify other areas which are considered to be of landscape importance. Suitable policies are needed for all these special areas, but there should be some distinction between those which are nationally important and those which are more locally important.

**Box 4.1 Local plan checklist for important landscapes**

Local plans should contain policies relating to the conservation, enhancement, and appropriate management of:

• nationally important landscapes

• other important landscapes

**Nationally important landscapes**

4.11 National Parks and the Broads, equivalent areas, and Areas of Outstanding Natural Beauty in England are designated by statute for the purpose of conserving and enhancing natural beauty (with the twin purpose, in National Parks only, of promoting enjoyment). Natural beauty is often broadly equated with scenic beauty, or more recently with landscape character and quality, but the statutory definition makes it clear that it also embraces flora, fauna, and geological features. It is now also commonly taken to include the historic environment. Heritage Coasts are non-statutory areas designated because of the high scenic beauty of stretches of undeveloped coast. The great majority of Heritage Coasts lie within areas also designated as National Parks or AONBs.

4.12 Government planning policy for National Parks and AONBs is set out in PPG 7. This states that conservation of natural beauty should be given great weight in planning policies for National Parks and should be favoured in those for AONBs. In both cases there should be special consideration of the environmental effects of proposals, while at the same time having due regard to the social and economic well-being of the areas. The PPG states that major development should not take place in National Parks or the Broads save in exceptional circumstances, and is normally inconsistent with the purposes of AONB designation.

4.13 Local plans should show the location, extent, and detailed boundaries for these areas and include appropriate policies for them which reflect the Countryside Commission's national policy statements. Such policies should indicate:

• the national importance of the area and the particular character and qualities that the designation seeks to protect

• that all development should, as far as possible, contribute to the natural beauty of the area

**Box 4.2 Example policy covering National Park, AONB, and Heritage Coast**

Hambleton District Council includes the following policy in its 1994 Deposit Draft, District-wide Local Plan:

L5:
The natural beauty of the Howardian Hills Area of Outstanding Natural Beauty and the Nidderdale Area of Outstanding Natural Beauty will be given the greatest possible protection and this will be given priority over all other planning considerations. Within or adjacent to these areas:

• any development which would adversely affect the natural beauty of their landscapes will be strongly resisted

• small-scale development required to meet the social and economic needs of rural communities will be permitted so long as such development is consistent with the protection of the natural beauty of the landscape and furthers AONB objectives

• small-scale tourist and outdoor sport and recreational developments will be permitted which are sensitively related to the distinctive landscape character and heritage of the area

• large-scale developments will be strongly resisted unless they are proven to be in the national interest, incapable of being located outside the AONBs, and designed to do as little damage to the environment as practicable

• where development is permitted, it must be of the highest standard of design and siting, reflecting the traditional character of buildings in the area and the landscape and normally using only local materials

• all proposals will be subject to a rigorous examination of their environmental implications. All proposals for large-scale developments likely to have a significant effect on the environment within the AONBs should be accompanied by an environmental impact statement.

- that major development should not take place in National Parks save in exceptional circumstances. Proposals should be demonstrated to be in the public interest and should be subject to rigorous examination. This should include an assessment of the need for the development, alternative ways of meeting that need, and environmental effects. In AONBs, major industrial and commercial development will normally be inconsistent with the aims of the designation. Only national interest and lack of alternative sites can justify an exception. PPG 7 sets out the assessment requirements in more detail.

- that small-scale development which is deemed essential to meet local community needs, and is provided for in the plan, is generally likely to be acceptable, but that account will be taken of the potentially adverse cumulative effects of such development, and emphasis will be placed on the importance of appropriate design.

4.14 Heritage Coasts are dealt with in PPG 20, *Coastal planning*, which indicates that policies to be pursued in these areas should be incorporated within development plans and should define the uses and activities which are or are not likely to be permitted.

4.15 The Countryside Commission has produced separate policy statements on National Parks, AONBs, and Heritage Coasts (see notes below). There is growing emphasis in all these areas on the use of landscape assessment to describe clearly the reasons for designation and the particular characteristics that need to be protected. Reference should be made in plan policies to the existence and value of such assessments.

4.16 Supporting paragraphs should also make reference to practical measures that are to be adopted for the conservation and enhancement of these areas, including, for example:

- participation in joint committees where areas span more than one district

- preparing, or contributing to, management plans

- setting up, or participating in, countryside management schemes or projects

***Notes***

*Countryside Commission policy on these areas is set out in the following publications:*

Fit for the future: the Countryside Commission's response to the National Parks Review Panel's report *(CCP 337), 1991*

Areas of Outstanding Natural Beauty: a policy statement *(CCP 356), 1991*

Heritage Coasts in England: policies and priorities *(CCP 397), 1992*

*Many designated areas are covered by a number of different planning authorities. National Park Authorities now produce a single local plan for each park. Where AONBs and Heritage Coasts are multi-authority, policies will need to be coordinated to ensure consistency. Management plans for these areas will give an opportunity to provide an overall statement of the relevant planning policies, as well as covering many other non-planning topics.*

**Other important landscapes**

4.17 Chapter 3 has indicated that we are placing increasing emphasis on maintaining diversity and distinctiveness of landscape character throughout the wider environment. We have also indicated, in paragraph 4.3, the DOE's wish to discourage proliferation of local designations. We nevertheless recognise that there may still be a desire, in some circumstances, to identify other areas of landscape importance (as distinct from the nationally important landscapes described above) for special policy treatment. We hope, however, that over time more sophisticated use and understanding of assessments of

**Box 4.3 Example policy on protection of locally important landscapes**

Hambleton District Council includes the following policy in its 1994 Deposit Draft, District-wide Local Plan:

L9:

Special attention will be given to the protection and conservation of the scenic quality and distinctive local character of the landscape in the areas designated as Special Landscape Areas on the proposals map and inset maps and normally this will be given greater weight than other planning considerations. Within Special Landscape Areas:

- development which would adversely affect the special scenic quality of the landscape will be strongly resisted

- small-scale development required to meet the social and economic needs of rural communities and small-scale tourist and outdoor sport and recreational development will be permitted provided such development is sensitively related to the distinctive local character of the landscape. Large-scale development will not normally be permitted.

- a high standard of design and siting in new development will be required reflecting the traditional character of buildings in the area and the landscape, and using materials sympathetic to the locality

- the conservation and maintenance of features important to the local landscape such as trees, hedges, copses, woodlands, and ponds, will be encouraged

landscape character may allow policies to be developed which are based on variations in character throughout the plan area.

4.18 In many cases local plans will inherit local landscape designations from structure plans, usually as either Areas of Great Landscape Value or Special Landscape Areas. Alternatively they may be identified as a result of a district-wide landscape assessment, usually on the basis of landscape types or areas which have strong, intact, and distinctive character, and special qualities and values that are considered particularly important. Historic landscape assessment will also have a growing role in identifying such areas.

4.19 When local plans do include policies for the protection of such areas they should be distinguished from those for the nationally designated areas. They should indicate what is special about the character and quality of the area and emphasise that appropriate development will only be permitted if it will have no significant adverse effects on these special characteristics. They should also identify the purpose of designation, including positive objectives and, where appropriate, specific targets. Mention should also be made, in the justification, of any practical steps that are to be taken to manage these areas.

## Sites, areas or features of nature conservation importance

4.20 PPG 9 states that the Government's objectives for nature conservation are to ensure that its policies contribute to the conservation of the abundance and diversity of British wildlife and its habitats, or minimise the adverse effects on wildlife where conflict of interest is unavoidable, and to meet its international responsibilities and obligations. It recognises that protection of wildlife habitat is the key to successful nature conservation on a range of sites. As a result of PPG 9 English Nature has revised its model policies for site protection. Few examples of these policies have appeared in plans as yet, and for this reason we use the model policies as examples in the following sections.

4.21 A wide range of areas or features has been identified as being of outstanding nature conservation importance, either because of their wildlife value or because they have special geological or geomorphological importance. Sites of Special Scientific Interest are identified by English Nature as representative examples of semi-natural habitats forming a nationally important set of sites. Some of them are also of international importance. Local authorities also designate local nature reserves and identify non-statutory sites of local importance for nature conservation. Both statutory and non-statutory sites need to be considered under policies for key environmental resources, as do matters relating to species protection.

**Statutory sites of international or national importance for nature conservation**

4.22 Sites of Special Scientific Importance (SSSIs) notified under the Wildlife and Countryside Act 1981 (as amended in 1985), are the most important sites in England for wildlife and earth science conservation. Some have additional international designations conferred on them. All SSSIs need to be firmly protected from development that would have an adverse effect on their special interest. These effects may be direct or indirect and it needs to be recognised that development outside the boundary of an SSSI can have serious repercussions within the area (for example, alterations to water tables, or the effects of water pollution some distance away). Local authorities need to consult with English Nature where there is a possibility of such indirect effects.

4.23 A number of the most important SSSIs are managed as National Nature Reserves, which English Nature owns, leases or manages by agreement. Marine Nature Reserves may also be designated by the Secretary of State to conserve marine environments.

4.24 Some SSSIs are of international importance, though the national legislation still provides the main mechanism for protecting them. Two significant international designations arise from Britain's obligations under EC Council Directives:

- Special Protection Areas (SPA) classified under Article 4 of the EC Council Directive of 1979 on the Conservation of Wild Birds

- Special Areas of Conservation (SAC) which are proposed to be designated under Article 3 of the 1992 EC Directive on the conservation of natural habitats, and of wild flora and fauna, and will become part of the European Natura 2000 network

In addition, there are sites of international importance listed under the Ramsar Convention on wetlands of

**Box 4.4 Local plan checklist for nature conservation**

Local plans should include appropriate policies or supporting statements to cover:

- protection of statutory sites of international or national importance for nature conservation
- conservation and enhancement of sites of regional, county or local importance for nature conservation
- protection of important earth science sites
- safeguarding protected wildlife species
- encouraging the management of features which are of major importance for wild flora and fauna

**Box 4.5 English Nature model policies for internationally and nationally important nature conservation sites**

**Sites of international importance**
Proposals for development or land use which may affect a European site, a proposed European site or a Ramsar site will be subject to the most rigorous examination. Development or land use change not directly connected with or necessary to the management of the site, which is likely to have significant effects on the site (either individually or in combination with other plans or projects), and which would affect the integrity of the site will not be permitted unless the authority is satisfied that:

- there is no alternative solution
- there are imperative reasons of over-riding public interest for the development or land use change

Where the site concerned hosts a priority natural habitat type and/or a priority species, development or land use change will not be permitted unless the authority is satisfied that it is necessary for reasons of human health or public safety or for beneficial consequences of primary importance for nature conservation.

**Sites of national importance**
Proposals for development in or likely to affect Sites of Special Scientific Interest will be subject to special scrutiny. Where such development may have an adverse effect on the SSSI, directly or indirectly, it will not be permitted unless the reasons for the development clearly outweigh the nature conservation value of the site itself and the national policy to safeguard the national network of such sites.

Where the site concerned is a National Nature Reserve (NNR) or a site identified under the Nature Conservation Review (NCR) or Geological Conservation Review (GCR) particular regard will be paid to the individual site's national importance.

Where development is permitted the authority will consider the use of conditions or planning obligations to ensure the protection and enhancement of the site's nature conservation interest.

international importance, especially as waterfowl habitats, known as 'Ramsar Sites'. As a matter of policy the Government has chosen to apply the same considerations to listed Ramsar sites as to SACs and SPAs.

4.25 PPG 9 sets out in detail, in Annex C, the procedures to be followed in development control in areas covered by EC directives. They require planning authorities to review existing planning permissions which may affect SPAs or SACs when they are consulted about these areas. The habitat regulations, which are now the main mechanism for protecting SPAs and SACs, restrict the granting of planning permission for development which is likely to affect these areas significantly and which is not directly connected with or necessary to their management.

4.26 Local plans should contain policies for the protection of all these internationally and nationally important areas. They should clearly indicate the circumstances in which development will or will not be permitted and should reflect the relative importance of different types of site. There should be particular emphasis on compliance with international obligations and protection of internationally important sites. Box 4.5 offers model policies which we believe would fully reflect these requirements.

**Sites of regional, county or other importance for nature conservation**
4.27 English Nature has endorsed the importance of other sites of wildlife, geological or geomorphological value which are not notified as SSSIs but are still considered to be important. Such sites are generally known as Sites of Importance for Nature Conservation (SINCs), although many different titles are used. They are being identified by many local authorities and are important because they are often highly valued by local people. Some sites may be Local Nature Reserves in that they are owned, leased or managed by agreement by the local authority under Section 21 of the National Parks and Access to the Countryside Act 1949, partly for educational purposes.

4.28 Policies should seek to safeguard these locally important sites wherever possible, and to minimise the effects of potentially damaging development. It will also be useful to indicate that where development is to be approved, appropriate measures will be required to protect the interest of the site, and/or to provide for compensatory benefits by enhancement and the creation of new habitats either elsewhere or on the site, using planning agreements where appropriate. For further information see English Nature's position paper on *Sites of importance for nature conservation* (1994).

**Protection of important earth science sites**
4.29 Local plans should give separate attention to the protection of earth science sites that are important for their geological exposures or features of physiographic importance. These sites are also often of great archaeological importance because of the early evidence that they can contain. Though supposedly dealt with under the broad heading of nature conservation, earth science interests are often forgotten in plans. The most important sites will be designated as SSSIs, and more

**Box 4.6 English Nature Model Policy on sites of local nature conservation importance**

Development and land use change likely to have an adverse effect on a Local Nature Reserve, a Site of Importance for Nature Conservation or a Regionally Important Geological/Geomorphological Site, or which would adversely affect the continuity and integrity of the landscape features listed below, will not be approved unless it can be clearly demonstrated that there are reasons for the proposal which outweigh the need to safeguard the nature conservation value of the site or feature. In all cases where development or land use change is permitted which would damage the nature conservation value of the site or feature, such damage will be kept to a minimum. Where appropriate the authority will consider the use of conditions and/or planning obligations to provide appropriate compensatory measures.

locally important ones are usually identified as Regionally Important Geological Sites (RIGS). There should be complementary policies for earth science sites which, as for wildlife, give the greatest degree of protection to the nationally important SSSIs, and a lesser, but still important degree of protection to RIGS.

***Notes***

*Further information on earth science conservation can be found in the former NCC's publication* Earth science conservation in Great Britain: a strategy *(1991).*

**Safeguarding protected wildlife species**

4.30 The role of local authorities in protecting species of wildlife is described in the Wildlife and Countryside Act 1981 (as amended in 1985) and in the consolidated Protection of Badgers Act (1992). PPG 9 gives guidance, in paragraphs 44 to 48, on the role of planning. Local plans should include a policy which states that the local authorities will not permit any development that would adversely effect any species protected by law, ie those listed in Schedules 1, 5, and 8 of the 1981 Act, species listed in Annex I of the EC Council Directive on the Conservation of Wild Birds and Annexes II and IV of the EC Council Directive on the Conservation of Natural Habitats and of Wild Flora and Fauna, and, of course, badgers. For more advice on badgers, see *Badgers on site - a guide for developers and planners*, produced by Berkshire County Council's Highways and Planning Department (1993).

**Box 4.7 Example policy on protected wildlife species**

Hambleton District Council includes the following policy in its 1994 Deposit Draft, District-wide Local Plan:

NC5:
Development will not normally be permitted which would adversely affect, directly or indirectly, animal and plant species protected by law. Where development is permitted the developer will be required to take steps to secure the protection of such animals and plants.

## Archaeology and the historic environment

4.31 PPG 15 is founded on the Government's belief that there should be effective protection for all aspects of the historic environment. Paragraph 1.1 states that the physical survivals of our past are to be valued and protected for their own sake as a central part of our cultural heritage and our sense of national identity.

4.32 Archaeological remains are irreplaceable and there is no doubt that the most important sites and areas, in both town and country, are a vital part of our 'critical environmental capital'. Many are already recognised for their importance and are designated as Scheduled Ancient Monuments (SAMs). Scheduling is not comprehensive, however. A great deal more remains to be discovered and plans should make provision for monuments which may be scheduled in future and for areas which are of potential archaeological interest. Nor is scheduling always the best form of protection for nationally important monuments. The appropriateness of its accompanying controls is often as much a criterion for scheduling as are measures of national

**Box 4.8 Local plan checklist for archaeology and the historic environment**

There should be policies in local plans to cover:

- preserving and enhancing internationally and nationally important archaeological sites or areas, with a strong emphasis on preservation *in situ*
- preserving and enhancing sites of regional, county or local archaeological importance, with a preference in favour of preservation *in situ*
- ensuring that areas of archaeological potential are properly evaluated and that where preservation *in situ* is not warranted there is proper recording prior to any damage or destruction of deposits
- conserving and enhancing important historic landscapes including historic parks and gardens and battlefields
- preservation and enhancement of conservation areas
- protection of listed buildings and their settings
- buildings or areas which are of local importance for their historical or architectural importance

importance. This is particularly so in towns, where the nature of urban archaeological deposits means that scheduling protection may be less effective than planning control. For all sites, whether scheduled or not, the local plan and development control are essential tools for protection.

4.33 It is not only individual archaeological sites which are important but, as indicated by PPG 15, the grouping together of archaeological or historic features within the broader historic landscape. Chapter 3 introduced the view that the whole landscape is to some degree historic, but it is also the case that some areas of historic landscape, or some specific features, will be considered to have special value and will therefore require special protection. Such protection is rarely provided effectively by scheduling, which is a mechanism best suited to individual sites or closely associated groups of monuments. Policies are needed both for archaeological features and for particularly important areas of historic landscape.

4.34 The most important parts of our historic built environment are also a critical part of the key environmental resources which plans must seek to protect. They make a major contribution to the character and quality of both rural and urban environments; their conservation is important for our quality of life, our links with the past, in helping to foster economic prosperity by providing an attractive environment to live in, work in or visit, and by encouraging inward investment.

4.35 Key parts of the historic built environment are designated by local authorities as conservation areas, and the most important individual buildings are listed. Many conservation areas and all listed buildings are considered to be of national importance and require suitable policies in plans for their designation, assessment, protection, and management. Local authorities also often identify important buildings or areas which are more locally important and policies for them may also be appropriate.

**Internationally and nationally important archaeological sites or areas**

4.36 In total, almost 20,000 archaeological sites or areas which are considered to be nationally important are already defined as Scheduled Monuments under Part I of the 1979 Ancient Monuments and Archaeological Areas Act. This is known to be an inadequate sample to represent the wealth of our archaeological heritage and English Heritage is involved in a programme known as the Monuments Protection Programme to continue to add ancient monuments to the schedule well into the next decade. Not all nationally important sites are or ever will be scheduled, however, and some nationally important remains will require protection by means other than scheduling. It is therefore important to recognise that there are many nationally important archaeological sites which are not scheduled but which still require protection.

4.37 A few nationally important archaeological monuments, buildings, and designed landscapes are also granted international status because they have been selected for inclusion in the UNESCO World Heritage List of historic sites and landscapes which are essential to a proper understanding of man's history in all parts of the world. There is no additional legislation to protect them but PPG 15 has now fully recognised their importance as key material considerations to be taken into account in development control. This relates to both the site and its setting. In accordance with PPG 15 plans should therefore include policies reflecting the universal value of these sites and setting out how they will be given appropriate protection, including a requirement for environmental assessment in the case of significant development proposals. Local authorities should also aim to prepare management plans for these sites, in conjunction with interested parties, which might act as a form of supplementary planning guidance.

4.38 Government policy on archaeology and planning matters is clearly set out in PPG 16, *Archaeology and planning*. English Heritage has also issued a separate leaflet on *Development Plan policies for archaeology*. We do not intend to repeat the content of these comprehensive documents here, but rather to draw out the key implications for local plan policies.

4.39 For nationally and internationally important sites, both scheduled and unscheduled, PPG 16 establishes a presumption against damaging development and in favour of preservation. The key requirement is that policies should aim, as far as possible, to prevent development which would adversely affect either the archaeological deposits or remains on or under the site or its character or setting, and should normally seek to ensure preservation of remains *in situ*. This approach should apply except in the most exceptional circumstances and reasons for departing from it must be extremely strong to counterbalance the national importance of the archaeology.

4.40 Known sites of this type should be shown on the proposals maps, but since knowledge is incomplete plans should also indicate that in assessing the archaeological effects of proposed development account will be taken of up to date SMR information, linked with application of the Secretary of State's non-statutory criteria for identifying monuments of national importance and the results of evaluations carried out by developers. The written statement will therefore need to make clear that not all archaeological constraints are shown on the map, and assessments of importance are likely to change with greater knowledge in the future. It may be helpful to show areas of archaeological potential rather than specific known sites, so that the map information is less incomplete. In urban areas, plans should make reference to urban archaeological assessment and strategies.

**Sites of more local archaeological importance**
4.41 As well as the monuments which are already scheduled, or which are known to be of national importance, there are many other sites or areas which are of more local importance. They may be significant within a region, a county, a district or even more locally, perhaps at parish levels, but cannot, at least on the basis of present knowledge and current understanding, be regarded as of national importance. These sites also require protection and in deciding on appropriate policies attention must be given to local values and perceptions. As with the other conservation interests of landscape and wildlife, however, there will need to be an appropriate differential in the degree of protection afforded to these sites in policies, compared with those that are of national importance.

4.42 Policies for these archaeological sites of more local importance should indicate that development may be refused unless it can be shown that it has no adverse effect on the special interest of the area. If development is permitted, on the basis of adequate understanding, then depending on the importance of the archaeological remains and the effect of the proposed development provision must be made for appropriate archaeological investigation and recording and compensatory enhancement elsewhere on site. All such sites may be included in one policy, although we recognise that some authorities may wish to distinguish between those of significance at a regional or county level and those that are more locally important.

**Box 4.9 Example policy on sites of archaeological importance**

Macclesfield Borough Council includes the following policies in its 1994 Deposit Local Plan:

BE23:
Scheduled Ancient Monuments and sites of county importance will normally be preserved. Development which would adversely affect such remains will normally be refused.

BE24:
Developments which would affect sites of district importance and areas of archaeological potential may be refused. Any proposal may require the submission by the applicant of an archaeological evaluation to assess the importance of the site. Development proposals must be designed to accommodate the archaeological remains where planning permission is granted.

BE26
Development which would affect other sites of archaeological interest not meriting preservation may be permitted provided that the applicant makes adequate provision for an agreed programme of archaeological investigation to take place.

4.43 In the same way as for nationally important sites, more locally important archaeological sites can, if possible, be shown on the proposals map, though perhaps as broad zones rather than individual sites. The written statement should point out that the map information is not definitive and indicate the other sources that will be used in assessing development proposals.

**Evaluating archaeological potential**
4.44 Archaeological knowledge is generally provisional and the precautionary principle is therefore particularly relevant. There are also many sites and areas which we know about, but whose level of importance is not yet fully understood. Equally there are many areas which may potentially contain important archaeological remains, but which have not yet been fully pinpointed or assessed. Planning decisions will need to be taken even though knowledge is incomplete. Risk can be minimised by consulting, for example, the County Archaeological Officer, or equivalent, and by following the guidance in PPG 16 on the use of field evaluation as a routine aspect of development control wherever there is reason to assume archaeological potential.

4.45 Local plans should therefore include a policy which indicates that where appropriate and necessary the prospective developer will be required to carry out a field evaluation to define the character and condition of any archaeological remains, the likely impact of development, and possible means of mitigating these effects.

**Providing for recording of sites and mitigation of development**
4.46 There will inevitably be some circumstances in which important archaeological remains will be affected by development and where it proves impossible or impracticable to achieve preservation of remains *in situ*. In such cases it is essential that appropriate archaeological recording takes place, and in many situations the developer should make appropriate provision for this.

4.47 Local plans should therefore also contain policies which will help developers, and other interested parties, to adopt appropriate procedures, recognising the need:

- for adequate information, based on field evaluation where appropriate, on the character and depth of deposits and on the impact of the development. This information is essential to allow informed decisions to be taken and should form part of the planning application. Applicants should be advised in the plan to seek appropriate professional advice at an early stage.

- to require mitigation, for example by design or redesign of development to avoid unnecessary damage to archaeological remains

**Box 4.10 Example policy on procedures for field evaluation and archaeological recording**

Cherwell District Council includes the following policy in its 1992 Deposit Draft Local Plan:

C27:
Before the determination of an application for development that may affect a known or potential site of archaeological interest, prospective developers will be required, where necessary, to make provision for an archaeological field evaluation. This evaluation should seek to define:

- the character and condition of any archaeological monuments or remains within the application site

- the likely impact of the proposed development on such features

- the means of mitigating the effect of the proposed development by redesign of the proposal to achieve physical preservation or, where this is not practicable or desirable, provision for archaeological recording prior to the destruction of the monument or remains

- to recognise that, in some cases, a mix of preservation *in situ* and appropriate investigation and recording may be required

- to provide for appropriate investigation and recording

**Protection of important areas of special historic landscape interest**

4.48 Although planning authorities should increasingly place emphasis on the wider historic landscape in its entirety (as in Chapter 3), there will still be circumstances in which local authorities will wish to identify specific areas of special historic landscape importance within which more focused policies may be applied. Wherever possible these should be integrated with areas of special scenic or nature conservation importance. Such areas may, for example, include interrelated groups of archaeological features, ancient woodlands, fields and field boundaries, and buildings, which together give a whole area of landscape a particularly important historic character. Areas of both single period and successive period types of landscape may be important.

**Historic parks and gardens**

4.49 Local authorities should give special consideration in their plans to the protection of gardens, parks and designed ornamental landscapes as places of special historic interest and value for recreation. Inclusion on English Heritage's *Register of historic parks and gardens of special historic interest*, though bringing no additional statutory protection, is confirmed by PPG 15 as a material consideration for development control purposes. Inclusion on the register indicates sites of national importance but local authorities may also wish to identify other more locally important parks and gardens.

4.50 Plans should include a policy which recognises the importance of sites on the *Register of parks and gardens*, and of other locally identified examples, and indicates that development which adversely affects their special historic character, or their setting, will not be permitted. Reference might also be made in the supporting text to the promotion of schemes for the repair, restoration or enhancement of parks and gardens.

4.51 Inappropriate development within registered sites should be guarded against, but there may be circumstances where appropriate and carefully planned development may assist conservation. Policies might usefully indicate that opportunities will be sought, through conditions or planning agreements, to achieve repair, restoration, and management of the landscape. Because of the sensitivity of registered sites, however, policies should emphasise that outline permission will not normally be given and that detailed proposals will be required before applications can be determined. A number of sources provide more detailed advice on

**Box 4.11 Example policy on historic landscapes and parks and gardens**

Hambleton District Council includes the following policy in its 1994 Deposit Draft District-wide Local Plan:

L8:
The character and features of the parks and gardens of historic or landscape interest, as shown on the proposals map and inset maps, will be preserved and enhanced, particularly those included in the National Register. Within parks and gardens of historic or landscape interest:

- development which would adversely affect their special historic character and appearance will not be permitted

- the conservation of their landscape and architectural elements will be encouraged

- the maintenance, restoration, and construction of traditional estate walling and fencing will be encouraged

- the restoration of their layout will be encouraged where this is appropriate and based on thorough and complete historical research

- development which would detract from their settings will not be permitted

historic parks and gardens, especially Annex 2 of PPG 15, the English Heritage leaflet *Planning and historic parks and gardens*, and a Garden History Society paper entitled *Advice on the protection of historic parks and gardens in development plans*.

**Historic battlefields**

4.52 After consultation, English Heritage has published a register of the more important and accurately located battlefields. It may be appropriate for local plans to show such sites on the proposals map and to include policies for their protection. PPG 15 confirms that inclusion on the register does not bring additional statutory controls, but the effects of development on such sites will be a material consideration in determining planning applications. PPG 13, *Transport*, draws attention to the need for new roads to avoid battlefields.

## Conservation areas

4.53 Government policy towards Conservation Areas is set out in detail in PPG 15. English Heritage has also set out its own advice in *Conservation Area practice*. PPG 15 notes that Conservation Area designation is the main instrument available to deal with conservation in neighbourhoods or areas. It stresses the duty placed on local authorities to formulate and publish proposals for the preservation and enhancement of Conservation Areas. It emphasises that it is particularly important for local authority policies relating, directly or indirectly, to development control in Conservation Areas to be set out in local plans, and for an indication to be given of the way that the plan relates to other documents or proposals for Conservation Areas.

4.54 PPG 15 also makes it clear that conservation (whether by preservation or enhancement) of their character or appearance must be a major consideration in Conservation Areas and that, although this cannot mean preventing all new development, the emphasis will need to be on controlled and positive management of change. Development proposals which would conflict with the objective of preserving or enhancing the character or appearance of a Conservation Area should not, on the basis of recent court decisions, be permitted other than in exceptional circumstances where there are issues of public interest.

4.55 Local plan policies will need to be framed with reference to the detailed content of both the PPG and the English Heritage advice. They will need to indicate the intent to preserve and enhance Conservation Areas and should show their extent on the proposals map. Local planning authorities have a duty to review their areas from time to time and we believe that policies should demonstrate a commitment to designate new Conservation Areas and/or extend existing ones, showing that this process will, where possible, be linked to the programme for reviewing plans. Designation can of course also be cancelled where the special interest that led to its designation has been lost.

4.56 Conservation Areas vary widely. It is increasingly recognised that it is the overall character of these historic areas which is important. The contribution of characteristics like the form and layout of buildings, the spaces between them, the influence of historic patterns of, for example, burgage plots or thoroughfares, the mix of historic and contemporary land use, the nature

**Box 4.12 Example policy illustrating approaches to Conservation Areas**

Hambleton District Council includes the following policy in its 1994 Deposit Draft District wide Local Plan:

HH1:
Development within or affecting the setting of a Conservation Area should seek to preserve or enhance all features which contribute positively to the area's character or appearance. Special regard will be paid to the impact of proposed development on the character or appearance of Conservation Areas, and development likely to have an adverse impact on that character or appearance will not normally be permitted.

HH4:
New development within or affecting the setting, character or appearance of Conservation Areas should comply with all of the following criteria:

- the position of the building on its site should relate to surrounding buildings and/or open space
- materials should be appropriate to the area and in keeping with the surrounding buildings
- the mass of the building should be in scale and harmony with surrounding buildings and the area
- the design of the building should ensure that the proportions of the parts are in scale with each other and relate to adjoining buildings, while detailing should be appropriate to the building and the locality
- the development should not adversely affect the streetscape, roofscape, skyline, and setting of the Conservation Area, or significant views in and out of the area
- the development should not adversely affect important open spaces as identified on the inset maps under policy BD5

In sensitive parts of Conservation Areas full applications will be required with detailed plans and elevations showing the new development in its setting.

of surfaces and details, and relationships to open spaces and important trees, are as important as the historic buildings that are present. Plans also need to recognise that Conservation Areas may have a strong archaeological dimension.

4.57 English Heritage places great emphasis on the need for local authorities to prepare Conservation Area assessments or appraisals. These are not a statutory requirement but PPG 15 makes it clear that the justification for designation, as reflected in such an assessment of special interest and character and appearance, will be taken into account by the Secretary of State in considering planning appeals in Conservation Areas. It is necessary for local authorities to carry out an assessment of their character which describes the special architectural and historic features which merit the designation of each one. Such assessments should be referred to in the plan, describing their role and importance and their use in development control. Policies should show that the local authorities will take steps to preserve the defined special qualities of these areas and enhance them where appropriate. The English Heritage leaflet referred to above provides guidance on the scope and method of such appraisals.

4.58 PPG 15 confirms a general presumption in favour of retaining buildings which make a positive contribution to the character or appearance of a Conservation Area. Local plans should therefore include a clear policy stating that demolition of such buildings or features will not be permitted. Although PPG 15 takes a more flexible stance, it is our view that demolition of other buildings, features or structures should only be accepted in cases where they are dangerous or incapable of repair – where real efforts have failed to sustain existing uses or find viable new uses, and where acceptable and detailed plans for redevelopment which will preserve and enhance the Conservation Area have been provided.

4.59 Policies should also indicate the local authority attitude to new development in Conservation Areas, stressing that this will only be acceptable if it is clear that the proposals will not detract from the special character and quality of the Conservation Areas. Special attention should be given to protection of trees, open spaces, designed landscape, and other features which contribute positively to the character of Conservation Areas. Because of the sensitivity of these areas, policies should demonstrate that outline permission will not be given and only detailed proposals will be considered. Policies should give encouragement to development proposals which will positively enhance Conservation Areas.

4.60 A policy should also be included stating that proposals for extensions or alterations will be permitted only if they are in sympathy with the character of Conservation Areas and that the local authority will introduce Article 4 directions if Conservation Areas are being adversely affected by changes taking place as a result of permitted development rights. Article 4 directions require the Secretary of State's approval and need to be backed up by clear assessments of the special architectural and historic interest of the area which demonstrate the importance of the features concerned.

4.61 As indicated in PPG 15, however, the Government now proposes to enable planning authorities to make directions withdrawing permitted development rights for a prescribed range of development materially affecting some aspects of the external appearance of houses in Conservation Areas. There will be no requirement to obtain the Secretary of State's approval for such directions, although the authorities will have to publicise their proposals and have regard to the views of local people.

4.62 In some circumstances in urban Conservation Areas it may also be helpful to include policies dealing with shopfronts, shop canopies, signs, and advertising where they have a potentially significant effect on the character of a Conservation Area. Policies may need to refer to supplementary design guidance on these matters.

***Notes***

*English Heritage is keen to emphasise the need for a selective approach by local authorities when defining new Conservation Areas, so that only areas with genuine historical or architectural merit are designated. Local authorities will need to refer in plans to their criteria for selection of these areas.*

*The character assessments or appraisals used to support local plan policies need to give a comprehensive account of the special character and quality of a Conservation Area, including the individual buildings, spaces, structures, landscape, and other elements, and of their groupings and relationships to each other. Further guidance on these appraisals is given in the English Heritage leaflet* Conservation Area practice.

## Listed buildings

4.63 Listed buildings are nationally important because they represent the best of our historic and architectural built heritage. PPG 15 describes them as a 'finite resource and an irreplaceable asset'. It establishes two particularly important principles relating to their conservation: firstly, a general presumption in favour of the preservation of listed buildings, and secondly, an emphasis on active use, usually an economically viable use, as the best way of securing their upkeep. It is therefore essential that local plans contain comprehensive policies which demonstrate the commitment of the local authority to the protection of the buildings themselves, their historic and archaeological value, and their settings, as well as to their sympathetic maintenance and repair. Appropriate

**Box 4.13 Example policy on aspects of listed buildings**

Ipswich Borough Council includes the following policies in its 1994 Deposit Draft Local Plan:

BE38:
Consent will not be granted for the demolition of a listed building other than in exceptional circumstances, and not unless the Council is satisfied that every possible effort has been made to continue the present use, or find a suitable new use. Demolition will not normally be permitted until there are approved detailed plans for redevelopment and development is about to commence. The Council will seek to ensure that demolition will be immediately followed by a continuous redevelopment building operation.

BE39:
The Council will seek to safeguard the character and setting of historic buildings through control of the design of new development in their vicinity, by control of the change of use of adjacent land to ensure that there is no adverse material impact, and by the preservation of trees and other site features as and where appropriate.

BE40:
Change of use of a listed building or a non-listed building of townscape interest will normally only be permitted if the applicant can demonstrate that the use proposed and any consequent alterations will not be detrimental to the structure, character, appearance or setting of the building.

BE41:
Applications for change of use of a listed building or a non-listed building of townscape interest which provide insufficient information to assess the impact of alterations associated with the proposed change of use will normally be refused.

BE42:
In considering proposals for external or internal alterations to a listed building, the Council will seek to ensure that there would be no adverse effect on its special architectural or historic character and appearance.

BE43:
In the interests of protecting the character and appearance of listed buildings the Council, in granting listed building consent (and planning permission where applicable), will seek to ensure that the loss or damage of historic fabric in the execution of the work is minimised.

policies should be formulated in the light of the detailed advice given in PPG 15 and especially the presumption in favour of their preservation. Care should be taken that any policies which are presented in the form of supplementary guidance are directly referred to in the plan.

4.64 All plans should include policies on all matters relating either directly or indirectly to development control decisions relevant to listed buildings They should be designed to prevent the needless demolition of listed buildings, or alterations which are not in sympathy with their special character. The factors to be taken into account in assessing proposals for the change of use or extension of a listed building also need to be clearly set out. Consent for demolition should only be permitted under very exceptional circumstances, and then only if it is clear that every possible effort has been made to continue the present use of the building or to find a sympathetic new use. It should also be a requirement that detailed plans for redevelopment are approved before such demolition is permitted and that a contract for the redevelopment is let before the work actually begins.

4.65 The fabric of listed buildings often has significant archaeological value. Local authorities should develop policies which are designed to ensure that, where appropriate, features which will be destroyed or lost during alteration or demolition will be recorded during the course of the work. Provision should be made for the deposition of such a record in an appropriate archive such as the NMR or the local SMR.

4.66 Other matters which will merit attention in policies include approaches to alterations, extensions, security measures, repair, change of use, and internal modification of listed buildings. It will often also be appropriate to cover matters like shop fronts, advertisements, and electronic and telecommunications equipment. It will be helpful for supplementary guidance to be provided on craft techniques, traditional materials, and details such as doors and windows.

4.67 Protecting the setting of listed buildings can be as important as retaining the special character and features of the building itself. Development within the curtilage, which would detract from the setting of listed buildings, should not generally be permitted.

4.68 Overall the aim should be to include an integrated set of policies which together will promote the protection and economic vitality of these important buildings, whether they are in towns or in the countryside. The emphasis should be on conserving their intrinsic character and maintaining their contribution to the wider environment. The maintenance of a Buildings at Risk Register and a resolution to use the Repairs Notice Procedure are other measures which could usefully be covered in the reasoned justification or supporting text.

## Other buildings of historic or architectural interest

4.69 Local authorities may also wish to identify, and include in their proposals map, other buildings, building groups or areas which they consider to be important at the regional, county or local level, but which are not formally defined as listed buildings or Conservation Areas. We support this and believe that plans should contain policies for them.

4.70 The nature of such policies will vary to reflect local circumstances but the aim should be to recognise the contribution of these buildings to the local environment, and to encourage their retention and appropriate repair and renovation. It may be helpful to refer, in the supporting justification, to a commitment to use building preservation notices in cases where proposals are made to demolish or carry out damaging work to an important unlisted building. This will allow time to decide if listing is appropriate.

**Box 4.14 Example policy on other buildings of historic or architectural interest**

Cotswold District Council includes the following policy in its proposed changes to the 1994 Deposit Draft Local Plan:

Policy 27:
Proposals will not be permitted for:

- the demolition or partial demolition of a listed building, except the removal of later modern additions which are of no historic or architectural interest, and where there is an overall improvement to the listed building or its setting
- the internal or external alteration or extension or change of use of a listed building, if this would in any way adversely affect its architectural and historic interest, or character, or setting
- the erection of a new building or other structure, or the use of land, where this would adversely affect the character or setting of a listed building
- the installation of satellite television dishes or other antennae, signs or other fitments, burglar alarms, solar panels, rooflights, and UPVC or aluminium doors or windows, on a listed building, where they would adversely affect its architectural or historic interest, or its character
- the removal of natural roofing materials from the roof slopes of a listed building, and their replacement with alternative modern materials
- the removal of traditional render or coloured limewash, where this is fundamental to the character of the building or the area
- the introduction of architectural features or materials removed and imported from another building, unless information is produced on the source of the feature and, if removed from a listed building elsewhere, evidence is produced that this was done with the benefit of listed building consent

The Council will act to halt the further decay of listed buildings at risk.

In cases where the demolition or partial demolition of a listed building is permitted, or where permission is given for the removal of features, the proper recording of the building will be required before any changes are made.

Proposals for alterations or changes of use to listed buildings will not be permitted, unless they are accompanied by sufficient information to enable a full and proper consideration of their effect. This will always include full survey drawings and, in some cases, photographs of affected areas. In exceptional cases, further information on the economics of the proposals may be required.

In areas where limewash or roughcast render are traditional, their reintroduction on listed buildings will be permitted where there is evidence that such finishes previously existed.

# Chapter 5 Promoting understanding and enjoyment and facilitating access

## Introduction

5.1 Enjoying and understanding the environment are important ways by which we come to value it more. Gaining access to our environmental heritage is one of the most effective ways of developing this enjoyment and understanding and there should be strong links between access and enjoyment, and conservation. PPG 17 on sport and recreation provides Government guidance on policy issues relating to access.

5.2 Although the integrated approach required for access and enjoyment is best dealt with in a non-statutory strategy, local plans can usefully set out a complementary framework. In particular, within local plans we are keen to see emphasis placed on:

- provision for recreation where it is close to demand, for example in the countryside around towns
- meeting the needs of different groups of visitors, for example by providing for local people, visitors, and those with special needs
- minimising private car use by providing opportunities for access close to where people live and to public transport links, and by promoting public transport as the best method of getting around
- managing and improving the public rights of way network (PROW), including National Trails, regional routes, local walks, and provision for horse-riding and cycling

5.3 We are also keen to promote:

- open access land as well as the public rights of way network
- the resolution of any potential conflicts between access and conservation objectives
- access to heritage features, appropriate information and interpretation, and maximum opportunities for environmental education

## The public rights of way network

5.4 The public rights of way network (120,000 miles of footpath, bridleway and byway in England) is the single most important means for people to enjoy the countryside. In 1993 some 20 million walks were taken in the English countryside, both by local residents and visitors (UK day visitor survey 1993).

5.5 The Countryside Commission's objective is to have the public rights of way network legally defined, properly maintained, and well publicised by the end of the century. The Commission is encouraging highway authorities to produce and formally adopt a strategic plan for achieving this national target – the Milestones Statement. The statement should clearly set out how much progress has been made towards the year 2000 target, what still needs to be done, and what resources are needed.

**Box 5.1 Local plan checklist for understanding, enjoyment, and access**

Topics we would wish to see covered in Local Plans are:

- policies on the public rights of way network
- the provision of new open access land
- policies on improving awareness and promoting understanding

5.6 Where it is particularly important that the PROW network is accessible and usable, district councils should ensure that the highway authority is aware of special areas, for example in the countryside around towns and in areas which experience visitor pressure, and that attention is given to them in relevant strategic documents.

5.7 The specific issues relating to rights of way which should be highlighted in local plans are:

- the value of the PROW network for local residents and visitors in enjoying the countryside
- endorsement of the highway authorities' commitment to attaining the national target
- local initiatives to open up, maintain, and promote the PROW network, eg Adopt a path, Parish Paths Partnership, development of regional routes

**Box 5.2 Example policy on the public rights of way network**

Warrington Borough Council includes the following policy in its 1993 Consultation Draft Local Plan:

OSR11;
The Borough Council will actively pursue the establishment of a network of recreational footpaths, particularly where these link green spaces to each other and increase the accessibility of open land to the urban areas.

- the need to safeguard existing ways which may be influenced by proposals for development

- the provision of new access opportunities in development schemes, with resources being allocated by the developer for the long-term maintenance of any such provision

- local authority criteria for new linear routes such as cycleways or horse riding routes, which may require land purchase or the negotiation of permissive access

***Notes***
*Policies within the local plan on transport measures and encouraging walking and cycling should be complementary to policies on the rights of way network (see Chapter 8).*

*Potential conflicts between public access and farming and between different users, eg cyclists, walkers, and riders, are best dealt with in a coordinated way, for example by a collaborative countryside management service or a Groundwork Trust project.*

***Further advice is available from:***
- *the Countryside Commission on the rights of way network generally and especially the publications on* National targets for rights of way: the milestone approach *There are an advisory booklet (CCP 435, 1993) and a statement (CCP 436, 1993).*

- *English Nature/English Heritage and County Archaeological Officers on access in relation to specific sites/areas of environmental importance*

- *voluntary groups including the Ramblers Association on walking, the British Horse Society and local riding groups on bridleways, and the Cyclists Touring Club on cycle routes*

## Open access land

5.8 Open access land where the public is allowed wider access on foot is a complement to the rights of way network. In the past emphasis has been placed on the creation of country parks. These still have a role, for example with the restoration of downgraded areas or the management of important landscapes or historic features, but much can be achieved by providing smaller sites or pocket parks strung out along the rights of way network, for example a picnic site or look-out point, a set-aside field or fields providing recreation opportunities. Local open spaces close to small towns and villages are particularly important.

5.9 Local plans should:

- contain policies protecting open access land from development

- indicate areas where the local authority will pursue the provision of further open access land

**Box 5.3 Example policy on open access land covering protection and additional provision**

Guildford Borough Council included the following policy in its 1993 Local Plan:

11R:
The Council will encourage, where appropriate and providing there are no adverse effects on the environment:

- the provision of suitably located facilities for informal recreation

- opportunities for increasing public access to open space

5.10 Mechanisms for creating access to land are wide-ranging. Most cannot be the subject of local plan policies but they include:

- securing sites and their long-term management in association with new development or as an after use for mineral workings

- the use of management agreements, for example under Section 39 of the Wildlife and Countryside Act, 1981

- various incentive mechanisms, including set-aside, Environmentally Sensitive Areas and Countryside Stewardship

- creation of community woodlands under the Forestry Commission's Woodland Grant Scheme

- agreements with Forest Enterprise to safeguard the freedom to roam

## Improving awareness and promoting understanding

5.11 Integrated programmes for access and enjoyment need appropriate information and interpretation for the general public and educational opportunities for schools and colleges. The public must be aware of the opportunities available for enjoyment of our environmental heritage and must be helped to have the confidence, ability, and understanding to make use of these opportunities in a considerate way.

5.12 Two elements of improving awareness are making available key sites where primary emphasis can be placed on interpretation and environmental education (these sites can act as gateways to introduce visitors to the environmental heritage of the surrounding area) and increasing the availability of information about the natural and built environment of the locality.

5.13 Local plans should:

- indicate the location of key sites to be promoted for environmental education

- indicate in the written justification the commitment which will be made to information dissemination

5.14 Key sites for education about wildlife will be local nature reserves and other similar sites run by the County Wildlife Trust, RSPB, etc. Those with on-site classrooms and warden/teaching staff will be particularly valuable. For many schools and other groups these key sites will be some distance away and accessible only on an occasional basis. Other sites are needed which although lacking special facilities are easily accessible. The target should be for every school to have a local nature site within 10 to 15 minutes' walk. Such sites could be owned by the local authority, or be subject to an agreement allowing access. A similar range of sites could also usefully be identified for the study of cultural history and historic landscapes. A wide range of techniques is available to give people better information about their local environment, ranging from leaflets and free newspapers to high-tech public access terminals linked to a computer database. Useful advice can be found in the Countryside Commission's policy statement *Enjoying the countryside: policies for people* (CCP 371, 1992).

**Box 5.4 Example policy on key sites for environmental education**

Nuneaton and Bedworth Borough Council included the following policy in its 1993 Local Plan:

E24:
An appreciation of the natural environment through the provision and development of resources for environmental education and community involvement will be promoted.

# PART III DEVELOPMENT TOPICS AND CONSERVATION INTERESTS

## Chapter 6 Transport

### Introduction

6.1 Transport policy lies at the heart of planning for sustainable development. According to the *National road traffic forecasts (Great Britain)* produced by the Department of Transport in 1989, road traffic will double or more in volume by the year 2025, with rural roads bearing a disproportionate part of this increase.

6.2 Road transport is a major contributor to global environmental concerns. It directly affects environmental quality at the local level through noise, vibration, pollution, and congestion. It leads to the requirement for new roads and road improvements, encourages increasingly sporadic development associated with activities seeking ready road access, and has resulted in a decline in public transport services which are essential to those without ready access to a car.

6.3 Without new measures to manage car use, global problems will increase and key elements of the countryside and built heritage could be squandered within a generation.

6.4 Against this background the publication of PPG 13, *Transport* (March 1994), represents a major turning point in transport planning. The guidance recognises the need to:

- manage the demand for transport
- coordinate policies for transport and integrate transport and land use planning
- promote planning and land use policies which reduce the need to travel
- encourage and support fully integrated transport systems, with proper provision for public transport, walking and cycling. It is recognised that the development patterns we set today will endure into the next century. 'If land-use policies permit continued dispersal of development and a high reliance on the car, other policies to reduce the environmental impact of transport may be less effective or come at a higher cost' (PPG 13, paragraph 1.10).

6.5 Through land use allocations and policies, local plans have a fundamental role to play in influencing the way in which people and businesses use transport. In turn, the land use allocations will reinforce or modify transport provision. Consistency is essential, therefore, between local plans and transport policies and programmes.

6.6 Local plans can also play a part in influencing road and transport proposals, through involvement with the County Council and by ensuring that adequate up-to-date traffic and environmental studies are carried out and that alternative transport strategies are investigated. Through the local plan process the environmental implications of certain road schemes can be assessed and local plans can influence, promote, and support measures initiated by others which reduce the environmental impact of travel and cars.

**Box 6.1 Local plan checklist for transport**

Within local plans we would expect to see:

- policies promoting land use patterns which reduce the need to travel
- policies on parking
- policies promoting walking and cycling
- promotion of public transport and support for integrated transport strategies
- promotion of traffic management in historic towns and cities
- promotion of traffic management in rural areas
- integration of transport and land use planning
- consideration given to the environmental effects of new road schemes

6.7 We fully support the thrust of PPG 13 and concentrate in the paragraphs below on those aspects of transport planning which are of most concern to us.

### Land use patterns which reduce the need to travel

6.8 Allocation of future land uses should aim to reduce the need to travel. This objective now lies at the heart of Government thinking on transport planning and development plans are central to it. Practical detail is set out in PPG 13, including the following principles:

- avoid decentralised, sporadic or dispersed development
- encourage development that makes full and effective use of land within existing urban areas

- without amounting to town cramming, especially land near public transport nodes and sites which are or could be easily accessible to facilities
- promote mixed uses as a means of encouraging people to live close to where they work and the services they require
- locate major new developments (including housing schemes, office development, and industry) adjacent to public transport services to encourage increased use, extension, and security of these services
- improve choice for people wishing to walk, cycle, and use public transport
- revitalise local centres in town and country and protect and enhance their viability and vitality
- achieve a balance in rural settlements between housing provision and employment opportunities to discourage the need for commuting
- locate freight-handling facilities where they can be served by sea/rail transport as well as road
- locate recreation facilities and develop new tourist attractions close to centres of population, in locations readily accessible to public transport

6.9 As a primary consideration during preparation of the local plan, these principles should underpin aspects of land use planning.

## Car parking

6.10 Land use policies which reduce the need to travel should be supported by other policies which reduce reliance on the private car. One of the most potent influences over car use is provision of car parking. From our perspective the provision of car parking also frequently causes damage to the setting, structure, and fabric of towns and uses sites which would be better used as town squares and open space. PPG 13 (paragraphs 4.4 to 4.11) provides considerable detail on parking, emphasising that in towns the aim should be to keep car parking provision to an operational minimum.

**Box 6.2 Example policy on land use patterns which reduce reliance on the private car**

Broxtowe Borough Council included the following policies in its 1994 Local Plan:

TR1:
Development proposals should utilise the most energy efficient and least environmentally damaging transport system.

TR4:
The Borough Council will encourage the use and development of public transport services. In particular, new developments for housing, employment, shopping or community facilities should normally be located and designed to enable the provision and convenient use of public transport services.

**Box 6.3 Example policy on reductions in parking provision**

Guildford Borough Council includes the following policies in its 1993 Local Plan:

5M:
The Council recognises that its car parking stock is of vital importance to the commercial activity of the town centre, but it does not intend to provide any additional car parks in the town centre as defined on the proposals map. It will maintain and improve the existing provision for short-term parking by management initiatives.

6M:
The Council will encourage appropriate initiatives, including park-and-ride systems, designed to meet the long-term parking needs of visitors to Guildford Town Centre. It will seek to satisfy such long-term parking requirements, and those of business commuters, in car parks planned in conjunction with public transport initiatives outside the defined town centre.

## Environmentally friendly forms of movement and integrated transport strategies

6.11 Walking and cycling are the cheapest, least damaging, and most easily accommodated forms of movement available and should be strongly promoted. This requires:

- land use planning to encourage the creation and retention of tight-knit mixed use developments which positively encourage walking and cycling
- providing routes and environments for walking and cycling which are safe, attractive, and direct

6.12 This is more fully covered in PPG 13 (paragraphs 4.12 to 4.18). Schemes in support of walking and cycling range from creation of new routes along canals, rivers, and disused railways, to using traffic management mechanisms to give pedestrian/cycle priority on certain roads and byways. In urban areas other options include provision of wider pavements and narrower carriageways, better road crossing facilities, and separation of cyclists from other road traffic.

6.13 Although public transport policy is not within the

**Box 6.4 Example policy on promoting walking and cycling**

Chorley Borough Council includes the following policy in its 1993 Deposit Plan:

T16(A):
The Borough Council will seek to ensure that major new development and transportation schemes incorporate facilities which encourage cycle and pedestrian movement. In particular the council will:

- require the retention or appropriate diversion of existing footpath and cycleway links within major new development and transportation proposals
- expect major development proposals to provide for pedestrian and cycle movement to nearby residential, commercial, retail, educational, and leisure areas, where appropriate
- seek where appropriate the provision of additional footpaths and cycleway routes between the countryside and built-up areas

direct control of local authorities, local plans in their written justification can lend strong support to public transport including, in some instances, making a commitment to subsidising services. As appropriate, local plans should also include specific land use proposals in support of public transport, such as:

- providing a sufficient density of development close to public transport nodes to ensure viability of the route
- allocation of sufficient land for car parking at bus and railway stations to encourage a modal shift in transport
- provision of new cycleway and footpath links to bus and railway stations, combined with bicycle lock-up facilities
- the safeguarding of routes, for example disused railway trackbeds, for possible future transport schemes including rail, metro, tram, and light rail projects
- ensuring that appropriate provision for public transport operations is made at the planning stage of new development
- encouraging the introduction of public transport services into new development at an early stage before travel patterns become established

6.14 Planning for environmentally friendly modes of travel in historic towns and rural areas is most likely to be successful if it forms part of an integrated transport strategy for a defined area. Such strategies should result in reduced congestion, improvement of the environment, and a lessening of need for further and potentially damaging road improvements. Integrated strategies are currently being encouraged by the Department of Transport, who wish to see them prepared for 'Strategic Units' (urban/rural) as part of local highway authority Transport Policies and Programmes (TPPs). This 'package approach' gives local authorities greater freedom to switch resources between different forms of transport. As a local highway responsibility, these strategies will normally be prepared at county level outside unitary authorities. Nevertheless, District Councils have a considerable role to play in their formulation. Where they have yet to be prepared, the written justification of local plans could usefully encourage their development and highlight areas where they are needed. There is no formal definition of a Strategic Unit for these purposes, but chosen catchments should be sensitive to traffic and amenity impacts beyond locally congested zones. This is particularly important given that the redistribution of traffic as a solution to congestion may create unforeseen changes in other places, even at relatively low additional traffic flows. Strategic Units are not conditioned by existing administrative boundaries.

## Traffic management in historic towns and cities

6.15 Excessive traffic and parking in historic towns and cities threaten the built fabric and people's enjoyment of it. Building facades suffer the consequences of air pollution, damage, and vibration, and historic street patterns may be destroyed or marred by more recent

**Box 6.5 Example policy on promotion of public transport**

Hambleton District Council included the following policy in its 1994 Deposit Draft District-wide Local Plan:

T21:
The provision of effective bus and rail services will be encouraged and proposals for improved public transport services which meet local needs for access to work, shopping, and community and leisure facilities will be supported. To this end:

- proposals for improved interchange facilities at Northallerton and Thirsk Railway Stations will be supported
- a site is allocated for a new bus terminus at the Auction Mart, Northallerton, as shown on the inset map

Proposals for public transport facilities will be required to incorporate appropriate access arrangements for people with mobility difficulties.

road schemes. Integrated transport strategies, for example those adopted for Oxford City, can do much to alleviate these problems. The mechanisms which can be employed as part of such strategies are many and various but can include street closure, pedestrian priority zones, traffic calming, a reduction in parking provision in city centres (potentially combined with increased parking charges), introduction or extension of park-and-ride schemes, bus priority measures, an extension of public transport routes and services, and introduction of new transport systems such as trams. Where integrated transport strategies have been prepared, relevant proposals should be incorporated in the local plan. Only land use proposals can be included in policy in local plans. Nevertheless, non-land use proposals, such as pricing mechanisms, might usefully form part of the reasoned justification for traffic management policies.

6.16 Even where an integrated strategy has not been prepared by the highway authority, local authorities could usefully include traffic proposals for city centres which lie within their responsibility, including provision for pedestrians and cyclists and a reduction in parking provision in town centres. Care is needed, however, to ensure that discouragement of cars in town centres does not encourage development in more energy-inefficient locations elsewhere, or push shoppers to more distant but less restricted centres. Equally, by displacing through traffic, city centre schemes should not lead to the need for a bypass.

The English Historic Towns Forum is collaborating with the Department of Transport in looking at innovative ways of achieving a more sensitive integration of traffic measures into historic townscape. A small number of experimental pilot projects will be pursued, based on the concept of historic core zones. These are to be mixed traffic areas giving greater freedom of pedestrian movement, where access by motor vehicles will be kept to a minimum and the use of control measures (signs, lines, road humps, etc) will be radically reconsidered to minimise their impact on the historic townscape. The facility of eventual adaptation of the existing regulations will also be considered, if this can be shown to bring significant additional benefits.

**Box 6.6 Example policy on traffic management in historic towns and cities**

Bridgenorth District Council includes the following policy in its 1994 Local Plan:

TT2:
The District Council will encourage the improvement of town centre environments through the use of pedestrian priority schemes, traffic calming measures, and the restriction of delivery vehicles to specific core times as well as providing rear servicing to premises where this is possible without damage to historic character.

**Box 6.7 Example policy on traffic management in rural areas**

East Lindsey District Council included the following policy in its 1993 Deposit Local Plan:

TR5:
Areas are identified where improved traffic management measures, possibly including pedestrian priority, environmental improvements, and car parking, are considered essential to the economic and social well-being of local businesses and residents...In addition the Council supports the need for speed limits on all roads through all villages and speed controls within residential estates. It will seek improved traffic management measures, including traffic calming, in urban residential areas and villages where through traffic is causing a danger to the local community.

## Traffic management in rural areas

6.17 Traffic management is also becoming necessary in rural areas, sometimes driven by traffic congestion but increasingly by wider concerns to sustain rural character while supporting combined environmental, social, and economic imperatives. Areas for management action are usefully identified in the plan process if, as is likely, the handling of traffic issues in one locality has a real or potential impact elsewhere. Mechanisms include:

- production of a clear 'road hierarchy' (at county level outside Unitary Authorities: see 6.14), in which roads are graded according to design and service levels
- traffic calming through villages
- minor roads and linking networks made safer and more suitable for non-motorised users
- speed controls either locally or area-wide, as in the New Forest
- careful location and use of car parks, based on demand management considerations (eg 'length of stay' charging, offering an incentive to leave the car for longer) as well as on revenue considerations
- community and post bus services
- school access arrangements including pick-up minibuses and safe cycling
- facilitation of general cycle use, including cycle hire at public transport nodes or within settlements, backed by repair and other support measures

6.18 In places such as the Lake District, specially signed 'Local Areas' have been proposed, within

**Box 6.8 Example policy on development associated with new transport links**

East Hampshire District Council included the following policy in its 1994 Deposit Draft Local Plan:

ENV12:
In order to protect open land adjacent to major transport routes, the District Council will not normally permit development which would adversely affect the conservation and maintenance of the local landscape.

which a coordinated set of traffic, transport, and community initiatives can be undertaken. Such coordination can serve the dual purpose of maximising environmental and amenity benefits while also offering a marketable image for the area. The mechanism here may be the preparation of a management programme for a traffic-managed 'Local Area'. This would be based on relevant proposals set out in the local plan, but framed in the wider context of the relevant Strategic Unit (see 6.14).

***Notes***
*Potential traffic calming measures include rumble strips, speed humps, and chicanes. In the North York Moors National Park, considerable success has been achieved by using cattle grids as a means of slowing down speed even where they are not strictly necessary. Where heavy goods vehicles are concerned, width reductions may be appropriate. Successful traffic calming schemes include those at Gamlingay (Cambridgeshire) and Buntingford (Hertfordshire).*

*The area-wide 40 mph speed restriction introduced in the New Forest on all non-major routes is indicated by regular signing and road markings, backed by clearly defined 'gateways' into the Forest. The result has been a significant drop in vehicle speeds.*

*The Countryside Commission supports experimental schemes for tourism traffic management in major recreation areas in partnership with local interest and tourist bodies: examples include local schemes in the Peak District, Surrey Hills AONB, and Purbeck. In addition, the Commission is running comprehensive traffic demand initiatives for the integrated rural and urban catchments of southern Surrey, the Lake District (Cumbria), and Dartmoor (Devon).*

## Integration of transport proposals and land use planning

6.19 As much as land use can influence travel patterns, so new transport infrastructure can influence development patterns. Transport proposals should be evolved in conjunction with the relevant development plan so that the interaction between transport provision and development can be fully addressed. This is rarely possible, because strategic transport links are prepared by different authorities and to a different time-scale from local plans. Nevertheless,

**Box 6.9 Example policy on the design of new road schemes/conservation of country lanes**

Hambleton District Council included the following policy in its 1994 Deposit Draft District-wide Local Plan:

T2:
Subject to policy L6 proposals for new roads and other improvements to the highway network which improve highway safety or bring about a net environmental benefit will be supported. The details of any proposal should seek to ensure that:

- the design of the scheme respects its surroundings
- adverse effects on residential amenity, settlements and their settings and the character or appearance of the countryside are minimised
- the best and most versatile agricultural land is conserved and farms are not fragmented unnecessarily
- there is no adverse impact on sites and buildings of architectural or historic interest, sites of nature conservation value or sites of archaeological importance
- the scheme provides for an integral landscape scheme to maintain and improve environmental standards
- the impact on public rights of way is minimised and adequate measures are taken to protect the safety and convenience of users
- pressures for future development which would be inappropriate are minimised

A full environmental assessment will be required for all major road schemes.

local plans need to be sensitive to these pressures and have a clear response to them (PPG 13, paragraph 5.10). Policy should indicate that development proposals relating to new transport links will be resisted unless the land in question is specifically allocated for development. Close attention will need to be paid to development pressure at motorway intersections and the pressure for warehousing adjacent to major trunk routes. Where relevant, local plans could also usefully identify the least environmentally damaging locations for motorway service stations (PPG 13, Annex A).

## The environmental effects of new roads and improvements

6.20 We are very keen to ensure that new transport links respect the environment and take full account of conservation issues (PPG 13, paragraphs 5.15 to

5.20). Although new strategic road routes are promoted through structure plans, we would encourage critical review of the environmental implications of local authority road schemes during local plan preparation. Bypass schemes, for example, may often have unforeseen environmental consequences, particularly where the line of the road subsequently serves also to define the limits of development for a settlement. According to paragraph 5.31 of PPG 12 if, during preparation of the local plan, it appears that a particular road scheme or its associated development would cause unacceptable damage to the environment, there is scope to consider its deletion or relocation, together with related changes in development, during the local plan inquiry.

6.21 Local plans should also take full account of local environmental constraints and characteristics when putting forward proposals for new non-strategic road links and improvements. The principles we would wish to see adopted and stated in policy are to keep road improvements on country lanes to an absolute minimum, recognising that such improvements can destroy their inherent character and increase traffic speeds to the detriment of walkers, cyclists, and riders (effectively restricting the use to motorised traffic).

6.22 Where essential road improvements are required, their impact can be minimised by:

- restoration of distinctive landscape features such as dry stone walls, banks, and hedgerows, and creative approaches to earthworks and geological exposures
- retention of old features such as setts and kerbstones
- avoidance of inappropriate additions such as pavements and street lighting
- maximising environmental gains within the corridor affected, including tree planting (PPG 13, paragraph 5.22)

# Chapter 7 Development for housing, commerce, and industry

## Introduction

7.1 Requirements for housing, commerce, and industry generate substantial demands for development which place significant pressure on the environment but which must be accommodated by local plans. Detailed Government guidance on planning to meet social and economic needs for housing, services, and employment while taking environmental considerations into account is well covered in a number of PPGs and it is not our intention to repeat it. Our advice focuses on their interface with our concerns for conservation, access, and enjoyment. It is particularly important to recognise that PPG 13, with its emphasis on reducing the need to travel and influencing the rate of traffic growth, will have a major influence on strategies for meeting development needs in the future.

7.2 Our major concerns relate to:

- general environmental considerations arising from different land use strategies, whether in town centre development, or on derelict or under-used edge of town, out of town or green-field sites
- specific issues relating to new housing and new commercial and industrial development

7.3 Reference should also be made to the many other sections of this advice which are relevant to such development, particularly the general principles relating to sustainable development, environmental assessment, and design (Chapter 2), the concerns relating to conservation and enhancement of the natural and built environment (Chapters 3 and 4), and those relating to transport (Chapter 6).

**Box 7.1 Local plan checklist for land use and environment**

We expect plans to contain:

- proposals and policies which contribute to quality of life and environment in urban areas
- proposals and policies based, as far as possible, on urban renewal and land recycling

## Land use strategies and general environmental considerations

7.4 Local plans can do a great deal to influence the environmental consequences of new development and help to direct it towards areas that are best able to cope. Allocations of land on the proposals map, and the policies which relate to them, can have major implications for energy use, transport, and service requirements, as well as for environmental and conservation interests. Choices about alternative strategies need to take full account of the full range of potential environmental consequences. Strategic environmental assessment will have an important role to play here. Major development for housing, commerce or industry is also likely to benefit from special attention to the need for project environmental assessment, as well as to general design considerations.

**Contributing to the quality of life**

7.5 Development and change do not have to result in a net loss for the environment. If properly planned and designed they can be a positive influence. Local plans should contribute to achieving this by ensuring that the general principles described in Chapter 2 are applied, especially with respect to environmental appraisal and design.

7.6 Policies and proposals in local plans can be designed to ensure that housing, industrial, and commercial development do not take place where they would adversely affect significant conservation interests. We expect local authorities to seek an environmental assessment where the development is particularly large in scale, or where it is likely to affect an area of special environmental sensitivity.

7.7 Design of new development of this type is very important. There are many examples of schemes which have made a positive contribution to their surroundings and the advice contained in Chapter 2 about design is relevant to all these forms of development, as are the comments about environmental benefits and planning obligations.

**Urban renewal and land recycling**

7.8 In general we believe that major new development should be based on a policy of urban renewal and land recycling rather than on new green-field development. This means that land allocations should concentrate on urban land which is derelict or despoiled and where high-quality design can make a contribution to environmental improvement. It is also important, however, to recognise fully that open land in towns and cities which may appear to some eyes to be derelict can have its own environmental value. Policies aimed at focusing development on such land should stress the need to recognise, and give proper weight to, its existing environmental and amenity value. Such land can contain:

- important urban green space which should be protected, including parks, green wedges, commons, river valleys, country parks, and local open spaces
- important sites for wildlife and earth science
- valued reminders of the past, which may include listed buildings, ancient monuments, and industrial and archaeological remains, as well as remnants of historic landscapes with their field patterns, old parish boundaries, and woodland

7.9 Policies need to recognise the dangers of 'town-cramming'. Some of our most vibrant urban areas are those which are tightly packed and full of character, such as the historic quarters of many cities, but nonetheless excessively dense urban development, and the associated levels of people and traffic, can contribute to a reduction in the quality of the urban environment and adversely affect local communities.

7.10 If development needs cannot be accommodated in towns and cities because the environmental capacity of the central areas is judged to have been reached in some way, then other strategies will need to be considered. Development on the fringes of towns may be an alternative in some areas where there is no Green Belt constraint. Where this type of development is proposed, special attention will need to be given to:

- the landscape setting of the town and the character and quality of individual areas of countryside
- the historic evolution of the settlement pattern
- the nature of the transition from town to country
- the character of the main approaches to the town and views to key landmarks from the surrounding area
- the value of open land adjacent to towns for wildlife, earth science, archaeology, and historical interest
- the importance of local countryside for access and enjoyment by local communities

7.11 Badly planned peripheral development can have damaging effects on the form, structure, and setting of towns and can detract from the traditional focus of the settlement. Such effects are particularly significant for historic towns.

7.12 In some cases it may be concluded that the only way to meet the need for new development is by allocation of green field sites beyond the edge of the existing urban areas. However, the concerns about transport implications addressed in PPG 13 mean that this is not a preferred solution. It will only rarely be a suitable strategy, where the need for the development is proven and where other alternatives have been fully exhausted. If a new settlement is considered, it is important to recognise that it must be big enough to be viable, and must meet employment and retail needs locally. There is certainly no general case for a change from the long-standing and widely accepted policy of resisting sporadic development in the countryside.

**Historic towns**

7.13 The issues outlined above can be especially important in historic towns. Such towns vary widely in character and in the planning problems that they face. Many are members of the English Historic Towns Forum (EHTF), which provides a means of exploring and tackling common problems.

7.14 The physical characteristics of historic towns are:

- a core with a tight physical fabric or a distinctive street pattern
- dominance by one or more historic landmark features
- a mix of uses and building types within a concentrated area
- a distinct physical location reflecting its origins (eg river crossing, defensive position, spa, seaside)
- a relatively limited spread of development beyond the core, giving a clear urban edge

7.15 Where local plans include historic towns, the policies and proposals will need to be carefully devised to find ways to accommodate necessary development without compromising the historic character of the town or its setting. No single solution will exist. Sometimes development in the centre will damage the historic core of the town, favouring development on the edge of the town centre or, though less desirably, on the outer periphery of the town. Elsewhere the setting may be so constrained that town centre development is favoured. In all cases, however, we believe in the need to maintain and foster mixed uses, in the interests of sustainable development, and as a means of ensuring vital and viable town centres. Single-use zoning limits activity to particular times of day, separates homes from workplaces, and inhibits the vitality and bustle that complement the character of the historic core and prevent crime. Many of these issues are addressed in the final report of the Chester research study, referred to in the notes following paragraph 3.64.

## New housing, commerce, and industry

7.16 Though many of the issues relating to these forms of development are outside our remit and are covered in detail in the relevant PPGs, some issues have an important interface with conservation interests.

**Box 7.2 Local plan checklist for new housing, commerce, and industry**

We would expect the following topics to be addressed:

- allocations of housing land that are based on environmental appraisal of alternative options
- policies for shopping that take account of the historic built environment
- policies for industrial and commercial development that take account of conservation interests

**Housing land allocations**

7.17 Local plans must ensure that, within the environmental constraints identified and taking account of demand management opportunities, adequate land is available for new housing. In identifying such land the need to conserve the natural and built environment is fully recognised. When local authorities set out to show land for housing on the proposals map, whether infill sites in smaller settlements or major allocations of housing land in or on the edge of towns, they should make sure that the alternatives are subject to environmental assessment which takes into account landscape character and quality, wildlife and earth science interest, archaeological and historic features, archaeological potential, townscape character, and local amenity and access.

7.18 In exceptional circumstances, for example in historic towns where the scope for town centre and peripheral development may both be limited, new settlements of varying sizes may be considered as the best solution to meeting housing needs, although the policy set out in PPG 13 means that the environmental transport implications of such proposals will increasingly rule them out. PPG 3 sets out the circumstances in which a new settlement may be contemplated. It makes clear that key environmental resources must be protected and that environmental benefits are desirable. It is essential that any proposals for new settlements should emerge through the development plan process, by identifying the most appropriate locations taking account of all other material considerations.

7.19 To assess possible locations for new settlements it is necessary to take account of the character and quality of the wider environment, including important features of landscape, wildlife, earth science, and archaeological or historical interest, as well as any nationally important designations. Areas of degraded landscape are likely to provide the best locations and will also offer the best opportunities for creative design and environmental improvement.

**Shopping**

7.20 Demand for new shopping schemes, both in town centres and in edge of town or out of town locations, is an important influence on towns and the countryside around them. Such schemes are having an increasingly significant effect on towns, and especially on the smaller market towns which largely escaped earlier pressures for redevelopment. Our main concern is that local plan policies should encourage retail developments which are appropriate in scale and character to their location. In historic town centres there should be an incremental approach to the planning of new retail development which, in general, should be of relatively modest scale and in keeping with the historic character of the town. Conservation Areas and listed buildings and their settings will need to be carefully protected. PPG 6 gives detailed advice on matters relating to shopping.

7.21 Designs will need to respond to the individual character and significance of the place and particularly:

- buried archaeological remains and the historic pattern and grain of streets, lanes, and alleyways, together with typical surviving back or burgage plots
- architectural styles of buildings, materials, shop fronts, and street paving and hard detailing
- appropriate form, scale, and bulk of new buildings
- associated requirements for servicing access and parking and the further effect that this may have on the environment

7.22 Although out of town schemes are now less likely to be favoured than previously because of transport implications we continue to be concerned about their effects. As well as being heavily reliant on car travel and so generating a significant number of car journeys their land take is also often extensive and can have adverse effects on important areas of open countryside near to towns, with potential repercussions for landscape, wildlife, and historical interest. They can also contribute to a decline in the vitality and viability of town centres, which can in turn lead to neglect of Conservation Areas, listed buildings, and other important historic features of the town.

**Box 7.3 Example policy on housing**

Guildford Borough Council included the following policies in its 1993 Local Plan:

1H:
The Council will seek to maintain and provide for a range of good quality housing, making the best use of scarce resources and minimising the environmental impact of development on green field sites.

7H:
In considering applications for new houses or replacement houses in urban areas, the Council will have regard to all relevant planning interests and particularly:

- whether the design is in scale and character with the area and avoids the adverse effects of overdevelopment
- the effect of development on neighbouring properties
- the effect on the existing context and character of the adjacent buildings and immediate surroundings

The Council will have regard to the environmental assessment of the urban residential areas set out in supplementary planning guidance.

**Box 7.4 Example policy on shopping**

Hambleton District Council included the following policies in its 1994 Deposit Draft District-wide Local Plan:

S3:
Retail development (Class A1 uses, Town and Country Planning (Use Classes) Order 1987) within the Town Centre Commercial Areas, shown on the inset maps, will be permitted provided that all of the following criteria are met:

- the traffic generated can be satisfactorily accommodated on the local highway network
- suitable parking and servicing can be provided
- the proposal will not have a serious adverse effect on townscape quality or local amenity
- the proposal will not result in the loss or unacceptable alteration to a building or feature of historic, architectural, archaeological or townscape interest
- the proposal will not result in an unacceptable loss of residential accommodation (see Policy H17)
- the proposal will not prejudice the use of upper floors (see Policy S7)

S9:
Outside the Town Centre Commercial Areas and the Secondary Commercial Areas in Northallerton and Thirsk, large retail developments will be permitted only when all of the following criteria are met:

- it can be demonstrated that there are no suitable sites for the proposal in Town Centre Commercial Areas or Secondary Commercial Areas. If there are no suitable sites within these areas developers should next look at the edge of town centres and in 'out-of-centre' locations last of all
- the proposal, either by itself or together with other such proposals or developments, will not seriously affect the vitality or viability of the centres of the market towns
- the proposal is of acceptable scale, materials, and design and does not have a significant adverse effect on the urban or rural environment or residential amenity
- the traffic generated by the proposal can be satisfactorily accommodated on the local highway network and the site can provide adequate car parking and servicing
- the proposal is sited so as to reduce the number and length of car journeys and can serve not only car borne shoppers but is also accessible to those on foot or who rely on public transport
- the proposal is within development limits
- a shopping impact assessment will normally be required to be submitted with any planning application for large-scale 'out-of-centre' retail developments

7.23 We believe that local plan policies should encourage shopping development which is accessible by a range of transport modes and which does not lead to an overall increase in car travel. Policies should be designed to try and strike the right balance between:

- encouraging town centre retail development of a scale, type, and design that will complement historic town centres
- accommodating edge of town or out of town shopping on suitable sites provided that, individually and cumulatively, this does not lead to a decline in the town centre
- using for shopping development derelict, disused or damaged land which has little or no conservation or amenity value and which lies outside or on the edge of the immediate town centre

**Commercial and industrial development**

7.24 Commercial and industrial development has considerable potential for adverse environmental effects. Land allocations again need to be based on careful appraisal of the alternative options, bearing in mind that business parks on the edge of towns raise some of the same concerns as out of town shopping centres in terms of generating travel by car. Locations which minimise travel should increasingly be favoured. Recycling of derelict or degraded land is likely to be particularly relevant for new industrial development, provided that the land does not have existing conservation interest.

7.25 New commercial development such as offices will often be located in or near to town centres. In some Conservation Areas this might, with good design, be in keeping with their original and historic character. In other areas with no tradition of commercial or industrial buildings, policies should ensure that such development takes place only in exceptional circumstances, for example where demolition of a building is to take place and redevelopment is considered to be appropriate. In all cases it will be vital to ensure that the highest possible standards of design are applied and that the development is in keeping with the special character of the Conservation Area. Where commercial development

**Box 7.5 Example policy on commercial and industrial development**

Warrington Borough Local Plan, Consultation Draft May 1993

ID1:
The Council will expect a high standard of industrial development and will require that all development proposals conform to the guidance outlined below and the Council's adopted standards:

- a safe, efficient, and attractive road layout and/or site access
- adequate space for the parking, manoeuvring, and loading/unloading of vehicles within the site to satisfy both operational and non-operational requirements
- adequate space within the site to meet foreseeable extension needs and to accommodate satisfactorily all external storage
- individual buildings should be of a good design and appearance, should be related to and compatible with any adjoining buildings, the area generally, and the natural features of a site in terms of environmental impact, siting, scale, mass, orientation, detailing, and materials
- recognition should be made of the importance of landscaping in terms of creating a pleasant working environment and reducing the impact of industrial development and of the need to design and treat means of enclosure as an integral part of the site development
- sites should be planned and laid out on a comprehensive basis in a neat, efficient, and visually pleasing manner with particular attention paid to the location and screening of storage and service areas and to the arrangement of car parks, buildings, and landscaping
- for industrial sites in close proximity to housing or recreational uses, landscaped or woodland 'buffer zones' should be provided along their more sensitive boundaries and consideration given to the use of other measures such as sound insulation, pollution control, and restricted hours of working. In order to minimise potential amenity problems use will normally be limited to Use Classes B1 and/or B8 in such circumstances.
- for schemes comprising a number of small factory units, communal vehicle circulation and parking facilities may be provided though each unit will still be required to have its own loading/unloading area

is likely to involve change of use and conversion of listed buildings, policies will again need to emphasise the need for careful attention to the special character of the building. Emphasis should be placed on criteria relating to height, density, design, scale, and relationship to the overall character of the built environment.

7.26 Policies should also aim to ensure that new commercial and industrial development does not adversely affect the character of other areas of historic or townscape value outside Conservation Areas, or buildings of historic importance which are not listed. Where former industrial buildings are to be converted for office use, careful attention should be paid to the potential value of the buildings and their surroundings for industrial archaeology as well as for their historic and architectural character. Inappropriate landscape treatment can also have a suburbanising effect on industrial areas.

7.27 Policies and proposals should be designed to encourage commercial and industrial development which:

- is designed to minimise energy consumption and is accessible by means of transport other than cars
- conserves existing features of value, including woods, trees, field boundaries, archaeological or historic features, semi-natural vegetation, and buildings of interest
- makes generous provision, in appropriate situations, for new planting to screen and integrate the buildings with their surroundings
- provides environmental benefits by creating new landscape features, new wildlife habitat or new access opportunities, as appropriate

# Chapter 8 Development in the countryside

## Introduction

8.1 We are committed to maintaining a diverse and environmentally healthy countryside which has thriving communities and is accessible to those who wish to enjoy it. We also recognise that complex forces increasingly influence the social and economic fabric of our rural areas and shape the rural environment. Although there has been substantial repopulation of rural areas, employment opportunities in traditional rural industries such as agriculture, forestry, and mining continue to decline. As a result there is a widely recognised need to diversify the rural economy in some areas in order to sustain rural communities and to provide the economic base to support the conservation of the countryside. We wish to see a positive response to these changes which recognises and reinforces the special character and quality of the countryside.

8.2 Rural development is covered in PPG 7. Our purpose in addressing this topic is not to repeat this Government advice but to highlight the matters which are of particular importance to our three agencies, focusing on the interface with our environmental remits and in particular expanding on aspects only touched on in the PPG. Our primary aim in considering development in the rural environment is to ensure that the special character and quality of the countryside, both inside and outside designated areas, are protected for future generations to enjoy. We believe that this means:

- supporting environmentally friendly farming practices which maintain and safeguard the natural and historic features of the countryside
- encouraging mechanisms to maintain landscape character and habitat diversity
- maintaining well balanced viable rural communities, and the built heritage which they support
- continuing to resist inappropriate new development in the open countryside

8.3 We welcome and support the rural diversification necessary to sustain the economic vitality which helps to maintain the countryside in all its aspects. This may be achieved through:

- farm diversification and alternative uses of land
- the creation of new rural businesses through the reuse of rural buildings
- the careful and sensitive addition of new economic development within and on the edge of rural settlements

8.4 All such development must be appropriate to its rural environment, however carefully located or well designed. It must take full account of environmental objectives as well as making a positive contribution to the local economy. To meet wider objectives for sustainability it should, as far as possible, be geared to the local labour market, thereby minimising commuting, and where possible be based on adding value to local materials and products, thereby helping to reduce haulage requirements. If this can be achieved there can be a fruitful partnership between rural conservation and rural economic development.

8.5 Not all rural change is subject to planning control, but local plans, notably the text which supports policies, give planning authorities a valuable opportunity to explain their broad strategy for the rural economy. Remoter rural areas, where the viability of farming communities is likely to be a matter of great concern, may need different approaches from areas closer to population centres and transport networks where non-agricultural employment is likely to be more common.

8.6 Diversification should reflect local circumstances, in terms of environmental constraints, local employment needs, and prevailing agricultural conditions within the area. Local plans could usefully distinguish between those economic activities which the local authority believes could make a direct contribution to the rural economy in harmony with environmental objectives, and those which may neither match local employment need nor meet environmental objectives.

**Box 8.1 Local plan checklist for development in the open countryside**

We would expect local plans to contain policies on the following topics, in all cases reflecting their interface with conservation interests:

- protecting the countryside from damaging development, both for agricultural reasons and for its own sake
- farm diversification
- reuse and adaptation of rural buildings
- new agricultural development
- agricultural and forestry dwellings
- horses and horse keeping

## Development in the open countryside

8.7 Despite changing circumstances, agriculture (as defined in Section 336 (1) of the Town and Country Planning Act 1990) still remains the primary land use that shapes and maintains the character and quality of the rural landscape. Below we concentrate on policies for the open countryside covering agricultural and forestry development and diversification and the reuse of buildings. Other aspects of rural diversification and development are considered in the second part of the chapter looking at village communities and in Chapters 6 (transport), 9 (infrastructure including energy generation from renewable sources), 10 (mineral and waste disposal), and 11 (tourism and active recreation).

## Protecting the countryside

8.8 With the exception of the most productive agricultural land (Grades 1, 2, and 3A: see paragraph 2.15), agricultural considerations alone no longer provide a sufficient basis for protecting the countryside, but PPG 7 makes clear the need to continue to safeguard the countryside for its own sake. This means protecting its landscape character, its nature conservation value, its historical and cultural significance, and its importance for access and enjoyment, and local plans will be central to this. The following points, discussed in detail elsewhere in this advice, bear repeating in the context of rural development:

- the use of landscape assessment to define the distinctive landscape character, both visual and historic, of different parts of a plan area may be particularly helpful in determining the scope for change in different areas (see PPG 7 paragraphs 1.2 and 1.14)

- nationally designated areas, including National Parks, AONBs, and other relevant designations, should be firmly protected from inappropriate rural development, but there should also be flexibility, to allow the safeguarding of character in the wider environment (see paragraphs 4.11 to 4.16)

- sites of Special Scientific Interest, Scheduled Monuments, listed buildings, and Conservation Areas should be firmly protected from damage and loss by development (see paragraphs 4.20 to 4.70)

- the nature and character of settlements and buildings should be a major determinant in considering the acceptability of new rural development

- access to and enjoyment of the countryside should not be compromised by rural development

**Farm diversification**

8.9 The changing Common Agricultural Policy is bringing land out of agricultural production and is leading farmers to seek to diversify their enterprises. Farm diversification can take many forms. Not all of them are subject to planning control, but new non-agricultural uses of land and the alternative use of farm buildings will require planning permission.

8.10 We accept the need for appropriate diversification if the countryside is to flourish and we also recognise the benefits which may arise in terms of:

- providing local employment and contributing to the local economy

- allowing farmers to take advantage of assistance for more environmentally sensitive land management, including non-intensive farming practices, woodland planting, habitat creation and management, and provision for public access and enjoyment

- maintaining farm viability and thereby enabling stewardship of the countryside by the farming community to continue

8.11 Appropriate diversification will, in the longer term, enhance the ability of the countryside to sustain itself. Ideally farm diversification proposals should contribute to the long-term maintenance of appropriate farming activity on the remainder of the unit, supporting environmentally sensitive farming practices wherever possible. Farm management plans could be the ideal framework for such

**Box 8.2 Example policy on protecting the countryside**

East Lindsey District Council included the following policy in its 1994 proposed amendments to the Deposit Local Plan:

DC1:
Permission for new development in the countryside as shown on the proposals and inset maps will only be granted where it can be shown that there is an overriding need for it to be in that location and when it can satisfy all other relevant policies and criteria in the plan.

In addition, all new development here will be required to:

- protect or enhance the particular character of the locality by its design, layout, and appearance

- protect grades 1, 2, and 3A agricultural land from significant loss (as defined by the Ministry of Agriculture, Fisheries, and Food's agricultural land classification)

- be constructed to a scale and form and in materials which are consistent with, or sympathetic to, the local character

- be accompanied by a landscaping scheme which shall show how adequately it can relate to its setting, how important natural features can be incorporated on and about the site, and how any elements of amenity or wildlife value can be enhanced

proposals, providing the opportunity to set out the future for the whole unit, incorporating matters such as habitat and landscape improvements, provision for public access, and the removal of unsightly development.

8.12 Some farm diversification can, however, have detrimental effects on the character of the countryside as a result of, for example:

- the introduction of new land uses out of character with the locality, including both permanent and temporary changes

- a change to enterprises which necessitate a clutter of temporary buildings, major new built development or the external storage of materials

- the gradual fragmentation of holdings, with separate small plots being released for hobby farming and horse keeping, sometimes to an extent which threatens the viability of the main farm enterprise

8.13 Against this background, we believe that farm diversification proposals should be assessed against the following criteria:

- they do not detract from the character and appearance of the locality and they meet with the environmental objectives of the development plan

- they will support the continuation of the farm enterprise as a whole

- they will not result in the inappropriate and unsustainable subdivision of the farm unit

- they will not result in the proliferation of new development under agricultural permitted development rights

- where appropriate they form part of an agreed farm management plan indicating the future use of other land and buildings on the holding

***Notes***

*A range of different policies within a local plan may have a bearing on diversification proposals. They include policies relating to buildings constructed under permitted development rights, building reuse, change of land use to sporting activities, increased indoor housing of animals, and horse keeping. These policies will need to be carefully integrated and suitably cross-referenced.*

*In some parts of the country, where there is heavy pressure for certain types of diversification, it may be necessary to have specific policies for different activities, such as garden centres and farm shops, especially where these may become major retail outlets.*

**Box 8.3 Example policy on farm diversification**

Hambleton District Council included the following policy in its 1994 Deposit Draft Local Plan:

EM16
Proposals for farm diversification will be supported provided all of the following criteria are met:

- the proposal is complementary to the agricultural operations on the farm and operated as part of the farm holding

- the character, scale, and location of the proposal are compatible with the plan's landscape and nature conservation policies

- the proposal does not adversely affect the best and most versatile agricultural land

- the likely level of traffic generated by the proposal is acceptable, taking account of the suitability of existing access and approach roads

- the scheme, where possible, reuses existing farm buildings

- where a new building is required it should be located within or adjacent to an existing group of buildings, be of a good standard of design and satisfactorily blend into the landscape in terms of design, siting, and materials

- the proposal will not bring about an unacceptable level of noise, air or water pollution

- the proposal will not have a significant adverse impact on the amenity of local residents

### Reuse and adaptation of rural buildings

8.14 A central plank of rural diversification strategy will be the continued beneficial use of the stock of rural buildings. Buildings suitable for conversion range from agricultural buildings to old mills and pump houses. Reuse provides a way of encouraging new economic activity without the requirement for new buildings in the countryside and we support this approach so long as the buildings have good access and can be easily serviced and so long as the use is of a scale and character appropriate to a rural location. Isolated properties will need to be given careful consideration. In all cases we believe local plan policy should indicate that such conversions must:

- not lead to the need for new development to house activities displaced by the conversion

- involve only buildings which are in harmony with their surroundings and do not detract from the setting of adjacent buildings

- involve only buildings which are structurally sound and do not require substantial rebuilding

- not disturb species protected under the Wildlife and Countryside Act 1981, for example, bats and barn owls

- provide for the retention or recording of archaeological or historic interest

- be in sympathy with the character of the building, and take particular care that major extensions, changes to roof lines, major rebuilding of external walls or external additions are not at odds with the building's existing character, original function, and contribution to local character

- provide employment opportunities primarily for people who live locally, thereby avoiding generation of substantial traffic movements or encouragement of reverse commuting from local towns

8.15 High priority should be given to the careful reuse of listed buildings and other buildings of historic importance, especially those of traditional vernacular character which have fallen into disuse, recognising that reuse of such buildings does offer a positive mechanism for ensuring their proper maintenance. Such buildings, in addition to being important in their own right, can contribute significantly to the landscape or to the character of settlements. The most sympathetic use of such buildings, however, is usually that for which they were originally designed. Where such uses remain, mechanisms should be found to encourage their continuation, including, perhaps, the conversion of other buildings to support the proper maintenance of a traditional building in its original use.

8.16 Where such uses no longer remain or are obviously no longer practicable, emphasis should be on finding alternative uses which call for only minimal changes to the structure and external appearance of the building (for example, by maintaining existing door and window openings). Light- or high-technology industry, craft workshops, certain tourism and recreational uses (for example bunk barns), and community uses are usually suitable uses.

8.17 For a variety of reasons we are not generally in favour of conversion of buildings, and especially those of historic importance, to residential use, whether for permanent or tourist accommodation. This usually requires the greatest change to the fabric of the building (such as creation of new window and door openings) as well as sometimes difficult subdivision of internal spaces and the addition of external works, such as gardens and parking areas, which can easily have a suburbanising influence on the landscape. The only circumstances in which we believe residential conversion should be acceptable are where:

- it offers the only means of retaining a valued building, and

- the proposed alterations to the building and surrounding curtilage do not damage the fabric of the building or significantly change its character

8.18 We are interested in all forms of traditional buildings, the small and relatively insignificant as well as the large. Whereas new uses can often be found for larger traditional buildings, smaller ones are often

**Box 8.4 Example policy on conversion to residential use**

East Hampshire District Council included the following policy in its 1994 Deposit Draft Local Plan:

ENV15:
The Council will normally only permit change to residential use when it can be shown that other uses have been explored fully and where it is satisfied that such a use is the only means of assuring the retention of the building.

**Box 8.5 Example policy on the reuse and adaptation of rural buildings to an economic end use**

East Lindsey District Council included the following policy in its 1994 proposed amendments to the Deposit Local Plan:

DC7:
The reuse of farm and other buildings in the countryside for commercial or community uses will be permitted provided:

- the form, bulk, materials, and general design of the existing building are in keeping with its surroundings

- the existing building is structurally capable of conversion

- it does not harm the character, amenities or appearance of the area or the amenities of nearby residents

- it would not cause traffic or access problems

- it does not substantially alter the form, setting, design or size of the existing building

- it does not result in the loss of habitat for protected species of wildlife

- it would not result in the dominance of non-agricultural uses in the countryside

- any outside storage forms a minor and ancillary part of the use and otherwise complies with policy EMP10

overlooked. We therefore wish to encourage the inclusion of these smaller buildings in sensitive schemes for economic reuse.

***Notes***

*The results of landscape assessment should help to highlight the types of building which are and are not suitable for conversion in different parts of a local plan area.*

*The written justification might indicate the willingness of the local authority to use conditions, as appropriate, for buildings subject to reuse (including Part 1 rights and Part 6 rights), when it is feared that the conversion of farm buildings will lead to construction of new farm buildings as permitted development.*

*Further useful reference material will be found in PPG 7 Annex D and in English Heritage's statement on* The conversion of historic farm buildings *(1993).*

**New agricultural and forestry development**

8.19 Environmentally friendly forms of farming and forestry are vital in sustaining the character and quality of the countryside. Local plans need to support sensitive agriculture and forestry, but they should seek to ensure that such development is in accordance with wider environmental objectives.

8.20 New farm development which requires planning permission includes large buildings, livestock units close to residential areas, and new development on units of less than 5 hectares. (Full details are given in PPG 7, Annex B.) Local plan policies on these forms of development should emphasise the importance of both the visual and historic character of the landscape in determining what is likely to be acceptable. Such developments should be assessed against the following criteria, which should be included in policies:

- they should be necessary for the purposes of agriculture or forestry on the unit
- there should be no unacceptable adverse impacts on landscape, wildlife, archaeological or historic interests
- they should be sited in or adjacent to the existing farm complex, and be sensitively located in relation to topography, other buildings of architectural or historic merit, and the sites of former farmsteads which may be of archaeological interest
- they should be sited close to an existing dwelling on the unit if the use of new buildings requires surveillance
- they should be in sympathy with the character of the locality in terms of design, materials, and construction
- they should be sited to take maximum advantage of existing screening

8.21 Where land fragmentation is a serious problem there would be merit in developing separate policy criteria for holdings under 5 hectares (see 8.20 above). Here a key concern may be to prevent suburbanisation of the countryside through the proliferation of development and/or intensification of use on adjacent small units.

**Box 8.6 Example policy on farm developments subject to planning permission**

Hambleton District Council included the following policy in its 1994 Deposit Draft District-wide Local Plan:

EM15:
Proposals for new agricultural buildings, which require planning permission, will normally be permitted provided that the following criteria are met:

- the building is located within or adjacent to an existing group of buildings, unless it can be demonstrated that a more isolated location is essential to meet the needs of the holding. Where an isolated location is essential the site should be chosen to minimise the impact of the building on the character and appearance of the countryside.
- in appropriate cases, the proposal is accompanied by an integral landscape scheme, reflecting the landscape character of the area
- the building is of a design which is sympathetic to its surroundings in terms of scale, materials, colour, and architectural detail
- the proposal will not have a significant adverse impact on the character or setting of local settlements or the amenity of existing residents
- the proposal will not have a significant adverse impact on sites of nature conservation value or archaeological importance or buildings of historic or architectural interest
- the proposal is compatible with the landscape policies of the plan

Normally a condition will be imposed to prevent the change of use of agricultural buildings to intensive livestock use.

8.22 Buildings for intensive livestock rearing, which are usually semi-industrial in design and operation, can be particularly intrusive, and if they are not handled with the greatest care can have a significant local impact. In areas where livestock rearing is common, local plans should include policies and criteria against which to assess such applications.

8.23 Under Part 6 and 7 of the GDO the majority of farm and forestry developments (excluding dwellings) are permitted development. However, certain types of agricultural and forestry development (including buildings, private ways, and excavation and deposits over 0.5 ha in extent) must be notified to the local authority prior to their execution. Where there is concern that the development will adversely affect visual amenity or sites of cultural, historical or nature conservation importance the local authority can require the submission of details of siting and appearance before the development can go ahead. This process, called determination, is fully described in PPG 7, Annex C. In this context we believe it would be helpful if local plan policies indicate:

- the circumstances in which the local authority is likely to request details on the siting and appearance of such agricultural and forestry developments for their approval

- the environmental criteria against which such developments will be assessed. These may be the same as those put forward for agricultural development subject to planning permission, but special criteria may be required for forestry roads.

***Notes***

*Design guides can prove very helpful in indicating to the farming community the design of agricultural developments which are acceptable in the local context. They can also form the basis of any discussions with farmers over individual development proposals. Reference should be made in plans to any supplementary guidance of this type.*

**Box 8.7 Example policy on agricultural and forestry permitted development rights**

Guildford Borough Council included the following policy in its 1993 Local Plan:

10RE:
When the erection, extension or alteration of an agricultural building or other works or excavations constitute development permitted under Class A of Part 6 Schedule 2 of the Town and Country Planning General Development (Amendment) (No. 3) Order 1991 but the Council determine that their prior approval is required by reason of sub-section A2 (Z) (A) of Class A of that order, they will not normally grant consent unless they are satisfied that the proposed siting, design, and external appearance of the building and the means of construction of the private way to it will not harm the countryside and the amenities of the locality.

*In the written justification local plans might indicate that planning conditions and obligations may be used to ensure that, where appropriate, suitable landscaping and screening are carried out as part of the development or used to achieve the demolition of unsightly dilapidated farm buildings which are of no architectural or aesthetic merit and which are not of special value for wildlife.*

*PPG 7 Annex B provides full details of planning control over agricultural development and Annex C provides full details of the determination process.*

**Box 8.8 Example policy on agricultural and forestry dwellings**

Cotswold District Council included the following policy in its 1994 Deposit Draft Local Plan:

11:
New agricultural or forestry workers' dwellings will normally be permitted, provided that all of the following criteria are met:

- an independent appraisal is submitted with the application, which shows clearly the functional need for, and where appropriate the financial viability of, the proposal

- the functional need for the proposed dwelling cannot be met by rearranging duties and responsibilities between workers

- the potential occupants can produce evidence of qualifications or experience in agriculture or forestry relevant to the nature of the application

- no dwelling has been sold from the holding by the applicant, nor any relevant occupancy condition removed from a dwelling on the holding or estate, in recent years

- the dwelling cannot be provided on a site within a development boundary, or on an approved development site, located where it would still meet the functional need

- the dwelling cannot be provided by rearranging, subdividing or extending an existing dwelling on the holding

- there are no existing, suitable, under-used buildings on the holding which could be converted to residential use

- there are no holiday lets on the holding which could be used to provide the permanent residential accommodation required, without significantly reducing the net income generated to the business as a whole

- where possible, the proposed dwelling is located within or adjacent to the existing farmstead, or other farm buildings on the holding

- the size of the proposed dwelling is appropriate to the functional need for it

**Agricultural and forestry dwellings**
8.24 There may be circumstances (although with a declining agricultural population this is increasingly rare) where there is a need to house essential agricultural or forestry workers outside settlements. Local plans should stress, however, the overriding principle of avoiding new housing development in the open countryside other than that which is essential for agriculture or forestry. Annex E of PPG 7 sets out the details of how such applications should be considered. Two matters are of particular concern to us:

- the potential for increased numbers of dwelling applications when farm holdings are subdivided

- removal of occupancy conditions from established agricultural or forestry dwellings which can encourage further applications for new dwellings

We are also keen to ensure that any new dwellings are associated with viable agricultural units.

8.25 Local plans should include a policy on such dwellings that stresses the strict environmental criteria that will be applied, and the requirement to prove the need for the building, in accordance with PPG 7. Such criteria should require that:

- a proven essential need cannot be met through available housing in the area, the implementation of an extant planning permission, or conversion of an existing building

- the development would be in keeping with the scale and character of the landscape and built and natural environment

- it would be sited close to other farm buildings

In addition, local plans should take account of the land use history of the holding as set out in Annex E of PPG 7, paragraph E12.

***Notes***
*Policies should always indicate that an occupancy condition will be imposed on new agricultural and forestry dwellings and that where appropriate an occupancy condition may be imposed on other dwellings used in connection with the holding.*

*The written justification or policy might indicate that where appropriate a S106 Agreement may be used to tie the farmhouse to adjacent farm buildings, or to the land of the unit, to try and provide a brake on fragmentation.*

*There is an increasing number of examples of dwellings with occupancy conditions which have been extended and improved through permitted development under Part 1 of the GDO. This can result in a dwelling which is no longer affordable by an agricultural or forestry worker. The plan might indicate that conditions can be used to remove Part 1 permitted development rights from new agricultural dwellings to ensure that they remain in their intended use.*

**Horses and horse keeping**
8.26 In recent years there has been a proliferation of pony paddocks and horse-related activities, especially in urban fringe areas and around some rural settlements. The use of land for recreational horse keeping can bring employment and economic benefits but can also have a significant impact on the countryside.

8.27 The grazing of horses for recreational purposes generally lies outside planning control, but beyond the curtilage of private dwellings associated development such as horse shelters and menage and turn-out areas is the subject of planning control. It is therefore valuable for local plans to include appropriate policies on horse

**Box 8.9 Example policy on horse keeping**

Hambleton District Council included the following policy in its 1994 Deposit Draft District Wide Local Plan:

SR11:
Proposals for development involving the keeping and riding of horses for recreation and/or commercial purposes, including stables, fences, jumps, and other equipment, will be permitted where all of the following criteria are met:

- the proposal is of a scale and nature appropriate to the character of the site and the ability of the local environment to absorb the development

- there will be no adverse impact on the character or appearance of the countryside

- buildings and structures are of a high standard of design and satisfactorily blend into the landscape in terms of their siting, design, and materials

- the amount of horse riding on or across roads that is likely to result will not have a detrimental impact on road safety and the free flow of traffic

- where appropriate, the proposal is located in an area with an adequate provision of suitable off-road horse-riding routes

- there will be no adverse affect on the amenity of residents in the vicinity or the enjoyment of other countryside users

- there will be no adverse effect on sites of nature conservation value or archaeological or historic importance.

Proposals in AONBs, Special Landscape Areas, Parks and Gardens of Historic or Landscape Interest, SSSIs, and the Green Belt will not be permitted where they are incompatible with the objectives behind these designations.

**Box 8.10 Local plan checklist for housing, villages, and the rural community**

We expect plans to include policies on the following topics, reflecting their relationship with conservation interests:

- maintaining the distinctive character of rural communities
- economic development in rural settlements
- housing development in rural settlements

keeping either where it is threatening local landscape character or where recreational riding is placing undue pressure on surrounding areas.

8.28 In developing policies on horse keeping, consideration needs to be given to the types of building which will and will not be acceptable in the local context. For example, some local authorities have taken the view that only field shelters (simple three-sided structures) are acceptable within the open countryside, whereas others consider that stables have no greater impact on the landscape and may actually encourage a higher standard of horse keeping which in turn should lead to better pasture management. The preferred solution is likely to vary according to local circumstances but any buildings need to be sensitively located and designed, taking account of the character of the landscape and any features of nature conservation or archaeological interest that may be present. Local authorities will also need to establish a view on the acceptability of other forms of horse-related developments, such as menage areas. The environmental impact of such developments will need to be weighed against their potential for reducing riding pressure on the surrounding countryside.

***Notes***
*Annex F to PPG 7 deals with development involving horses. The Countryside Commission booklet* Horses in the countryside *(CCP 261, issued in revised form in 1993) also includes relevant information.*

## Housing, villages, and the rural community

8.29 The environmental quality of the countryside, combined with ease of movement, has made villages attractive for many people who are no longer in rural employment. Provision of employment, housing, and services in rural areas is of great importance socially and economically. We are particularly keen to ensure that:

- housing provision is balanced by local employment opportunities and other services, so that village communities can be relatively self-sufficient (this is one of the concepts positively promoted by PPG 13)
- the special character and quality of rural villages are maintained

**The character of rural communities**
8.30 All development in rural settlements needs to be seen within the context of each settlement's physical and social or cultural character. Physical character depends on location and setting, historical evolution, building materials, and styles, and the grouping and arrangement of buildings, roads, open space, and landscape features. Socially and culturally, villages increasingly fall into one of two categories: those lying close to major employment centres which are largely dominated by commuters and have very little local employment, and those in remoter areas which in the past have largely been dependent on agriculture, forestry or the minerals industries but now suffer from a lack of employment opportunities and an ageing population.

**Box 8.11 Example policy relating to the character of rural communities**

Hambleton District Council included the following policy in its 1994 Deposit Draft District-wide Local Plan:

H8:
Within the development limits of villages residential development will be permitted where it involves infilling, conversions or small-scale development or redevelopment and where the development meets all of the following criteria:

- it will not result in the loss of or damage to spaces identified as important to village character under Policy BD5
- it is of a scale, density, and layout appropriate to the size and form of the village
- it is of a design which in terms of propositions, materials, and architectural detail is sympathetic to the vernacular character of the village and the locality
- it will not create unacceptable highway problems
- it provides a satisfactory standard of residential amenity and has no significant adverse impact on the amenity of neighbouring properties
- it will not have an adverse effect on areas or buildings of historic or architectural interest, or sites of nature conservation value or archaeological importance
- it will not have an adverse effect on the character or appearance of the countryside
- it will not result in the loss of land of recreation or amenity value identified under Policy SR1

8.31 There are now many examples of villages, especially commuter settlements, which have suffered from both extensive infill of poorly designed housing and new village-edge housing, often in the form of small estates, which are unrelated in design to the village vernacular styles. This has severely eroded the character of these settlements and increased the sense of suburbanisation in areas which are essentially rural. At the same time, the cultural distinctiveness of many rural settlements has been diluted by emigration of the indigenous population in search of work and immigration of newcomers seeking their rural idyll. This has sometimes been exacerbated by too rapid housing expansion, largely to the benefit of incomers.

8.32 Against this background our key environmental concerns are that:

- the distinctive character of individual rural settlements should be maintained
- the environmental capacity of individual settlements to accept further change should be carefully assessed

Local plans should identify the scale and pace of change that can be accepted within the individual villages of the plan area without diluting or destroying their physical or cultural character, and indicate the location of sites where new development can be accommodated without compromising environmental interests. The emphasis should always be on maintaining a balance between economic activity and residential provision. Where it is concluded that certain rural villages have reached their capacity, the pressure for essential new development should be diverted to those settlements which have the capacity to absorb further change without harm to the environment.

**Economic development in rural settlements**

8.33 Diversification strategies should aim to improve employment opportunities in rural settlements, particularly in areas where they can help sustain and be serviced by an existing local population. Employment growth which necessitates substantial commuting by car or further inward migration of people to rural areas should be avoided.

8.34 Employment opportunities may be provided by the conversion of existing buildings, as already discussed, or, on occasion, by providing new premises within and on the edge or rural settlements. The location of such new development should be carefully considered in relation to the character of rural communities and should meet strict environmental criteria requiring that the development is:

- of a scale and type appropriate to the locality, its social character and the appearance of the settlement and surrounding countryside
- of a design and style which reflects the local vernacular, including use of local materials, as appropriate

Such criteria will need to be applied particularly strictly in designated landscapes, although we recognise that it is critical to ensure the viability of rural communities in these areas. It will be important to avoid the high cumulative social and environmental impact of a series of commercial uses which individually would have relatively minor impacts.

**Box 8.12 Example policy on economic development in rural settlements**

East Lindsey District Council included the following policy in its 1994 proposed amendments to the Deposit Local Plan:

MP3:
Within or next to a settlement, the council will normally permit industrial development on land not specifically allocated for industry provided:

- the development and associated infrastructure does not cause air or water pollution or otherwise harm the amenities of the area due to noise, dust or fume emissions or traffic generation
- its times of operation can be controlled
- its size, scale, layout, design, materials, positioning or appearance does not harm the character of the area
- it satisfies a local employment need which cannot be met on a site allocated under Policy EMP2 or complies with Policy EMP4

**Housing in rural settlements**

8.35 Provision of housing to meet local needs has an important role to play in maintaining rural communities and should be covered in local plan policies. Under the Rural Exceptions Scheme mechanisms can be made available in rural areas to secure special low-cost housing sites outside settlement limits and outside general housing allocations. Although we recognise the importance of such provision, it should not be allowed to compromise the environmental objectives of the plan, as even a few houses in the wrong place can have a lasting adverse impact on landscape and settlement character. Historic settlements are especially vulnerable to the effects of even a few houses in the wrong place. We believe that the need for affordable housing should be met as part of development schemes on sites allocated for housing in the development plan. This may be assisted by specifying affordable housing quotas on particular development sites. Only when this mechanism fails to meet the identified need should ‘exception schemes’ be considered.

**Box 8.13 Example policy on housing in rural settlements**

Guildford Borough Council included the following policy in its 1993 Local Plan:

10H:
Exceptionally, the Council will give favourable consideration to granting planning permission for the provision of affordable housing for local needs in rural areas, provided that all of the following criteria are met:

- the Council is satisfied that the scheme would meet a genuine need that would otherwise not be met
- the site is within or adjoins a settlement as identified on the proposals map
- the site does not exceed 0.4ha
- the type of housing is all affordable housing for local needs on a permanent basis
- the development of the site would take full account of environmental considerations
- the Council is satisfied that the settlement and infrastructure are adequate and additional public resources will not be required to improve services
- the development of the site will not conflict with the purposes of the Green Belt or adversely affect the open character of the Borough's countryside

It should be noted that any permission granted will need to be regulated by formal arrangements to achieve the objective of providing permanent affordable housing for local needs.

8.36 Policies should clearly indicate that affordable housing schemes will be acceptable only if:

- a genuine local need is proven by means of a properly conducted survey, and there are adequate arrangements to ensure that its status as low-cost housing can be maintained for future occupants
- the proposal takes full account of environmental interests and does not have unacceptable adverse effects on the local landscape, on archaeological or historical interests, on wildlife or on the character of the settlement

Wherever possible such schemes should form a logical extension to settlements and should demonstrate appropriate use of materials and design, in keeping with the character of the area.

# Chapter 9 Infrastructure requirements

## Introduction

9.1 In this chapter we consider infrastructure requirements other than transport which are needed to support development and which impinge on our areas of concern. The topics dealt with are energy, water supply, and communications.

## Energy

9.2 Electricity generation from fossil fuel is the single largest contributor to the production of greenhouse gases in the UK and is a primary contributor to acid rain. Actions at all levels are required to address these global issues and, as acknowledged in PPG 12 (paragraphs 5.9 and 6.11), development plans must consider policies that have the potential to reduce Britain's contributions to these problems. In this respect our two primary concerns are to see policies which encourage energy conservation and encourage sensitive development of renewable energy sources.

### Energy efficiency

9.3 The White Paper *This common inheritance* promoted energy efficiency improvements as the cheapest and quickest way of combating the threat of global warming. Energy conservation and improved energy efficiency are fundamental to sustainable development and should be the central plank of any energy policy. Although many aspects of energy conservation lie outside land use planning, certain aspects directly relate to land use and should be encouraged in local plans. These include:

- support for recycling measures which can result in considerable energy savings (see Chapter 10)
- encouragement of district heating schemes and combined heat and power schemes, wherever practicable, subject to amenity considerations
- energy-conscious siting, layout, and orientation of new buildings including avoidance of hilltop or windy sites
- the enhancement of local micro-climates through the use of tree belts and tree planting to reduce wind speeds and trap air between buildings, perhaps incorporated as planning conditions

**Box 9.1 Local plan checklist for energy**

Within local plans we would expect to see policies on the following topics, in all cases reflecting their interface with conservation interests:

- promotion of energy efficiency
- sensitive development of renewable energy
- the transmission and distribution of electricity

(Refer also to Chapter 6 on transport and energy conservation.)

9.4 In supplementary design guidance every opportunity should be taken to promote the use of energy conservation measures, passive solar design (the harnessing of solar energy by appropriate design), and active solar energy technology (solar panels) in the design of new buildings and in the conversion of existing buildings.

**Box 9.2 Example policy on energy conservation and efficiency**

Thamesdown Borough Council included the following policy in its 1994 Deposit Draft Local Plan:

TEV76:
The Council will look favourably on proposals that seek to optimise reduction in energy consumption by means of layout, design, construction, and alternative technology. In considering such proposals the Borough Council will have particular regard to the design and conservation policies in this local plan.

### Renewable energy

9.5 As set out in Energy Paper 62 *New and renewable energy: future prospects in the UK*, the Government wishes to stimulate the exploitation of renewable energy sources wherever they have the prospect of being economically attractive and environmentally acceptable. *This common inheritance* set a target of 1000 MW (later increased to 1500 MW) of electricity-generating capacity from renewable sources by the year 2000. Use of renewable energy resources has been encouraged by the Non-Fossil Fuel Obligation (NFFO) introduced under the Electricity Act 1989. This places a statutory obligation on regional electricity companies to contract for a minimum of non-fossil fuel generating capacity. Although primarily aimed at providing a market for nuclear power, it also supports renewable forms of energy generation.

9.6 As set out in PPG 22 *Renewable energy* (paragraph 25), local plans should include detailed policies for developing renewable energy sources and should identify broad locations, or specific sites, suitable for the various types of renewable energy installations. Renewable energy sources offer great benefits in addressing global concerns, but it is also necessary to give the fullest attention to their consequent environmental effects. With regard to our particular areas of interest we are conscious that:

**Box 9.3 Example policy on wind turbine generators**

Hambleton District Council included the following policy in its 1994 Deposit Draft District-wide Local Plan:

UT6:
Proposals for small individual wind turbines, not intended to supply power to the electricity grid, will be permitted subject to the criteria listed below.

Wind farms, groups of wind turbines or large individual wind turbines will not normally be permitted within or where they would have an adverse affect on the AONBs, SSSIs, scheduled ancient monuments, registered parks and gardens of special historic interest and the Green Belt.

In the Special Landscape Areas, parks and gardens of historic or landscape interest, and sites of nature conservation value, wind farms, groups of wind turbines or large individual wind turbines will only be permitted if it can be shown that the proposal would not adversely detract from the special amenity, landscape, scientific or historic interest of these areas and there are no other suitable sites in less sensitive areas.

Elsewhere, proposals for wind farms, groups of wind turbines or large individual wind turbines will be supported provided that:

- by itself or together with other such proposals or developments in the area it will not significantly affect the character or appearance of the countryside
- the wind turbines and any other structures or buildings are of a high standard of design and satisfactorily blend into the form and pattern of the landscape
- it will not have an adverse impact on the character or setting of settlements
- it will not lead to a significant nuisance to the public arising from noise, safety, shadow flicker, electro-magnetic interference or reflected light. Wind turbines will not normally be permitted within 400m of a dwelling unless it is part of a development supplied by that turbine.
- it will not cause unacceptable highway safety problems and no permanent access roads are built to or across the site
- the power lines required to link the wind turbines to the electricity grid or user buildings are provided underground where they would cross sensitive areas
- it does not adversely affect a listed building, a conservation area or a site of archaeological importance
- there is no adverse impact on public rights of way or the recreational enjoyment of the countryside
- redundant turbines, plant, transmission lines, and access roads will be removed and the sites restored

- the primary renewable resources of wind and water tend to be in the coastal areas and uplands which are also some of the most sensitive landscapes, many designated as a National Park, AONB or Heritage Coast
- renewable energy generation, although clean, can directly affect substantial areas for what is generally a relatively small power output. For example, to supply 10% of Britain's current energy needs using on-shore wind power would require an estimated 30,000-40,000 wind turbine generators covering a land area of 1500-3250 sq km under present technology.
- biomass coppicing could influence large areas of land and have a significant impact on landscape character

9.7 Against this background we hope that local authorities will give careful consideration to where renewable resources can be exploited without causing undue environmental damage within their area.

**Wind energy**

9.8 In line with Government guidance on renewable energy sources (paragraph 9.6 above), local authorities at county or district level have a real opportunity to take an environmentally led approach to the siting of commercial wind turbines by assessing where they can best be located without damaging important and sensitive resources. As the primary impact of wind turbines relates to landscape, such an appraisal should be underpinned by a systematic landscape assessment of the plan area.

9.9 Wind turbines are often sited in highly visible hill- or ridge-top locations. The cumulative visual impact of a number of wind turbine generators or wind farms concentrated in a locality is of particular concern, but noise and vibration may also be significant within 0.5km of generators. On present evidence, the long-term impact on wildlife can be minimised, although wind turbine generators may disturb bird nesting patterns and migratory flight paths, and foundations and underground cabling may alter local hydrology, which may be a specific concern on peat.

9.10 We believe that wind turbine power stations supplying the national grid should be subject to a hierarchy of acceptability. It is our view that there is no overriding national need for wind turbine power stations to be located in designated areas. Therefore, such developments should not be allowed in or adjacent to the existing and proposed conservation designations of national importance covering World Heritage Sites,

National Parks and the Broads, equivalent areas, AONBs, Heritage Coasts, SSSIs, Scheduled Monuments, and registered parks and gardens and battlefield sites.

9.11 In the wider countryside, wind turbine power stations should be allowed only where the prospective developer can clearly establish that the proposal would not adversely affect the value of the site or the character of the surrounding landscapes.

9.12 The criteria, wherever possible informed by a landscape assessment, which should be used when assessing the appropriateness of wind turbine power stations in the wider countryside include:

- that scale and siting (by itself or cumulatively with other development) do not have a significant adverse impact on landscape quality or recreational enjoyment
- the need for a high standard of design, incorporating the necessary mitigation measures to minimise impact on the surrounding landscape
- that account is taken of the routing of any power lines serving the development (see 9.16 below)
- avoidance of:

  intervisibility with other wind turbine generators

  the setting of Conservation Areas, areas of archaeological interest, and listed buildings

  highly visible skylines

  the habitats of protected species

  migration flyways or significant flight paths of birds

  major wintering/staging areas for birds, especially waterfowl

  fragile habitats which would be significantly adversely affected by the proposal, for example peatlands

9.13 We believe that support should normally be given to the development of small, non-commercial wind turbines in the countryside (including designated areas) so long as they are designed and located to avoid conflict with landscape, historical, and wildlife conservation interests, and their cumulative effect does not detract from the visual amenity of the countryside. Local authorities could usefully provide separate design guidance on the domestic use of renewable energy sources.

***Notes***

*In local plans, policies relating to wind energy will need to cross-refer to policies covering the protection and conservation of the environment, with particular reference to policies relating to statutorily designated areas.*

*Central Government guidance on wind energy is set out in PPG 22,* Renewable energy. *This guidance acknowledges that special care should be taken in assessing proposals for developing renewable energy projects in National Parks, AONBs, the Broads, and SSSIs, and that similar considerations arise in areas of archaeological or historic importance and on the coast (paragraphs 27 to 29).*

*We believe local authorities should press for an environmental assessment of all those wind turbine power station proposals in their area likely to have significant environmental effects.*

*Useful references include: the Countryside Commission,* Wind energy developments and the landscape *CCP 357 (1990), and the Countryside Council for Wales* Wind turbine power stations *(1992).*

**Transmission and distribution of electricity**

9.14 Major power lines can be highly intrusive in the landscape, especially where they follow geographical features such as river valleys or ridges. Their size is also out of scale with the setting of historic settlements and Conservation Areas and will be particularly intrusive where a number of power lines converge. For these reasons, although appreciating their national necessity, we would wish to see policies in local plans which seek to prevent the further development of major power lines in National Parks and the Broads, equivalent areas, AONBs, Heritage Coasts, registered parks and gardens and battlefields, and in close proximity to Conservation Areas, listed buildings, and Scheduled Monuments.

9.15 Planning authorities have only a limited role in determining applications for erection of major overhead lines, which are the responsibility of the Secretary of State for Trade and Industry. Nevertheless, if location within these areas is unavoidable we would seek policy statements which require either that the lines are placed underground or that the final overland route is chosen following careful

**Box 9.4 Example policy on power lines**

The Yorkshire Dales National Park included the following policies in its 1995 Draft Deposit Plan:

LC7:
In situations where new overhead utility service lines would be prominent, the National Park Committee will, subject to technological and operational constraints, seek their placement underground or the least visually intrusive alternative overhead route. It will also encourage the undergrounding of existing overhead services wherever practicable.

LC9:
The National Park Committee has no direct control over high voltage overhead transmission lines and any undergrounding or rerouting of such lines can only be achieved with the agreement of the electricity supply company.

landscape assessment of the alternative options. Policies on power lines will need to cross-refer to others covering the protection and conservation of the environment, especially those relating to statutory designated areas. In some situations, it may also be appropriate for plans to contain policies promoting undergrounding of existing overhead lines in sensitive locations. Useful additional information can be found in the Countryside Commission's position statement *Overhead electricity lines: reducing the impact* (CCP 454, 1994).

## Water

9.16 Our demand for water is steadily increasing. In some parts of southern and eastern England this demand has outstripped supply, with over-abstraction of water from natural aquifers and from rivers themselves, contributing to greatly reduced river flows and falling water tables. The outward manifestations of this have included long sections of once-perennial rivers drying up for years at a time, the drying of lakes which were once the focal point of historic designed landscapes, and the drying out of once ecologically rich floodplain meadows, to the detriment of landscape, wildlife, and the setting of historically important landscapes and settlements.

9.17 These problems are primarily the responsibility of the National Rivers Authority and the water companies, but they are also of concern to local authorities, and they directly impinge on our areas of interest. We are particularly concerned that land use decisions should not result in:

- the further exacerbation of current low flow problems
- the development of new, environmentally unsympathetic, water supply resources to meet demand

9.18 We would therefore encourage local authorities to view the availability of potable water as a potential constraint on new development and to encourage demand management of water where the development of new water resources would be to the detriment of conservation interests.

**Water as a planning constraint**

9.19 In parts of southern and eastern England the task of supplying water to new developments is becoming increasingly onerous and threatens to result in further over-abstraction. In line with NRA thinking we believe that new developments should be concentrated in areas where adequate water resources already exist, or where new provision of water resources can be made without adversely affecting the water environment or other conservation concerns, or where demand will not lead to new reservoirs. This type of policy should be developed in close liaison with the NRA and if necessary be cross-referred to policies for river valleys or river catchments.

**Box 9.5 Local plan checklist for water**

Within local plans we would expect to see policies that:

- stress the availability of water as a planning constraint
- place emphasis on reducing the demand for water and managing local resources in a sustainable manner

**Box 9.6 Example policy on water supply as a planning constraint**

Warrington Borough Council included the following policy in its 1993 Consultation Draft Local Plan:

DC3:
The Council will not normally permit development which increases the requirement for water unless adequate water resources either already exist or will be provided in time to serve the development and without detriment to existing abstractions, to water quality, fisheries, amenity or to nature conservation.

**Demand management of water**

9.20 Even if policies are successful in guiding new development to areas where adequate water resources already exist, rising water demands per household and infilling within existing settlements will still require the planning of new strategic water resources such as the construction of new reservoirs or the transport of water over long distances. The development of such resources could have considerable environmental impacts. We believe it is important for local authorities to signal in their written justification that where new water supply resources are proposed, the local authority would wish to be satisfied that this provision is essential and could not be avoided through mechanisms aimed at reducing the demand for water, such as metering.

## Telecommunications

9.21 PPG 8 recognises that over the next ten years or so, various aspects of telecommunications may prove to be among the most potent forces in enabling a reduction in car use by increasing opportunities for home working. Telecommunications may well expand the opportunities for diversification in the remoter parts of the countryside. For these reasons we support the development of the telecommunications network. Such developments, however, can have an impact on the environment. In this respect our particular concerns are:

- the potential proliferation of telecommunication antennas in historic villages and urban centres, in Conservation Areas, and on listed buildings
- the construction of telecommunication masts and towers in prominent or sensitive locations within designated areas which, coincidentally, may also be sites of historic importance

**9.7 Local plan checklist for telecommunications**

Against this background we would expect local plans to include policies on the following topics, reflecting the need to respect environmental constraints:

- telecommunication developments subject to permitted development rights
- telecommunication developments requiring a planning application

**Permitted telecommunications developments**
9.22 Local authorities are able to exercise some control over the siting and appearance of certain telecommunication development permitted by the General Development Order. Such permitted development is subject to a prior approval procedure (paragraphs 21 to 24 of PPG 8).

9.23 In accordance with PPG 8 (paragraph 16) we would support local plans which indicate where particular attention will be given to the siting and appearance of permitted telecommunication developments eg in relation to listed buildings and their settings, Conservation Areas and their settings, the settings of ancient monuments, the settings of archaeological remains, and developments within historic designed parks and gardens. Policies relating to permitted telecommunication developments may need to cross-refer to policies relating to such areas and sites. Wherever feasible and appropriate we would encourage screening of equipment housing by planting or landscaping. Local plans may usefully indicate in the written justification circumstances in which Article 4 directions might be used, to withdraw permitted development rights (PPG 8, paragraphs 18 to 19).

**Telecommunication development requiring a planning application**
9.24 In the case of telecommunication developments subject to full planning control we accept that, for technical reasons, some of these facilities may have to be in prominent or sensitive locations to meet operational requirements. Nevertheless, we believe that they should not normally be permitted in or adjacent to designated areas (including National Parks, AONBs, Heritage Coasts, Grade 1 Historic Parks and Gardens or within the setting of ancient monuments and Conservation Areas) unless it can be demonstrated that:

- no alternative, less intrusive, technically acceptable solution exists
- the development provides an essential link in a national network

9.25 For all telecommunication developments, regardless of location, local authorities should indicate in their local plan the other criteria which would be used in judging the suitability of individual telecommunication proposals. Our primary concerns are to:

- minimise the proliferation of telecommunication developments by encouraging site sharing or mast sharing wherever feasible
- minimise ancillary developments in the open countryside
- maximise the opportunities for landscaping and screening to reduce the visual impact of this type of development

In local plans, policies relating to telecommunication developments may need to cross-refer to policies covering the protection and conservation of the environment, especially those policies relating to statutorily designated areas.

**Box 9.8 Example policy for telecommunication development**

Hambleton District Council included the following policy in its 1994 Deposit Draft District Wide Local Plan:

UT4:
Proposals for telecommunication developments, such as masts or other structures, will not be permitted within or in locations where they would have an adverse effect on AONBs, Special Landscape Areas, parks and gardens of historic or landscape interest, SSSIs or other statutory nature conservation sites unless they would provide an essential link in a national network for which no alternative sites exist. In such cases measures will be required to minimise any adverse impact.

Elsewhere proposals for telecommunication development will be permitted provided that all of the following criteria are met:

- there will be no serious adverse effect on the character or appearance of the area
- it can be demonstrated that existing masts or structures cannot be used for the purpose
- it is not located within a conservation area or would detract from the setting of such an area or a listed building
- there would be no unacceptable adverse impact on residential amenity

# Chapter 10 Minerals and waste disposal

## Introduction

10.1 Mineral extraction and waste disposal as landfill can lead to considerable and irreversible change in landscape character and loss of wildlife habitat over large tracts of land. It is not only the direct effects of these operations which are of concern to us, but the indirect effects which can affect considerable areas, such as change in water table levels associated with mineral extraction and landfill, leading to deterioration of water-dependent habitats and waterlogged archaeological deposits, and pollution of groundwater by landfill leachates. The cumulative and on-going impact which may be associated with the concentration of mineral workings in specific areas is of special concern. On the other hand we recognise that many abandoned mineral sites now provide oases for wildlife and well conceived restoration plans can be of positive benefit in some landscapes.

10.2 These issues are a local plan matter, even though prepared at county level. They are therefore considered in some detail below.

**Box 10.1 Local plan checklist for minerals**

We are particularly keen to see the following points addressed in statutory plans:

- policies on reducing demand for primary minerals
- consideration of environmental capacity in mineral planning
- planning for future after-use
- policies on restoration and aftercare
- policies on earth science interest

## Minerals

10.3 Sustainability objectives require attention to be focused on limiting demand for primary minerals both by the use of secondary aggregates and recycled materials, and by influencing development options and designs to limit demand for building aggregates. The use of recycled materials and secondary aggregation is now a central theme of government guidance, as set out in MPG 6 paragraphs 32 to 39. We also believe that emphasis should be placed on:

- the use of environmental capacity to establish acceptable limits to mineral extraction
- the coordination of the after-use of mineral workings with other environmental policy objectives for the plan area
- the highest standards of restoration and aftercare
- the recognition that archaeological remains are a finite and irreplaceable non-renewable resource
- pursuing earth science considerations, through seizing opportunities for creating new geological exposures by carefully designing extraction and restoration

### Reduction in demand for primary minerals through recycling of mineral wastes and use of substitutes

10.4 Policies which give every encouragement to the recycling of mineral wastes, the recycling of waste materials from the building industry, and the use of substitute materials should be central to mineral planning, with the aim of reducing the need for new mineral workings. This is of particular relevance to the peat and aggregates industries. In the case of peat, recycling and composting schemes are some of the most direct ways in which district authorities can make a direct contribution to the conservation of peatlands. In the case of aggregates, recycling may have the added benefits of assisting in the reclamation of derelict land which has excessive waste materials and in reducing the amount of industrial waste requiring disposal in landfill sites. Some waste mineral tips are now of considerable wildlife interest, including a number of SSSIs. Such tips should not be disturbed. MPG 6 paragraphs 28 to 39 are important references on this topic.

### Environmental capacity in mineral planning

10.5 Conservation and other environmental issues should be prime considerations in identifying potential areas for mineral extraction. We would expect mineral extraction to avoid nationally designated areas except in cases of pressing national need (see MPG 6 paragraphs 70 and 71).

10.6 MPG 1 *General considerations and the development plan system* states that minerals plans should indicate in

**Box 10.2 Example policy on the recycling of mineral wastes**

Kent County Council included the following policy in its 1993 Minerals Local Plan Construction Aggregates Written Statement:

CA5:
The County Council supports the use of substitute and recycled materials and, when dealing with such proposals, will normally give permission for their import, reworking or processing, subject to the location being acceptable and to the impact of the operation being acceptable within the terms of policies CA16 to CA23.

appropriate detail those areas within which there will normally be a presumption for or against mineral working. Various factors are listed which should influence these decisions, among which we believe a key determinant should be the environmental capacity of an area to yield minerals without leading to a decline in overall environmental character and quality. Identification of environmental capacity should include setting finite limits or phased thresholds on the release of land for different minerals. The concept of phasing is important, because although an area may not be able to accept the rapid change associated with a number of active workings occurring in close proximity both in time and space, it may be able to accommodate a number of changes over an extended period so long as these do not involve the loss of rare environmental resources. Assessment of environmental capacity will need to be based on plan policies for all aspects of environmental conservation and enhancement, including definition of key environmental resources.

10.7 In fact, the concept of environmental capacity to some degree already contributes to the identification of 'preferred areas', expressed as a series of environmental overlays or constraints, which define areas where mineral working would and would not be acceptable. County- or district-wide assessments of landscape character can make a useful contribution to this. Our concern, however, is that local authorities may be expected to achieve set targets for mineral production regardless of any environmental thresholds identified, although as acknowledged in MPG 6 (paragraph 58) the preparation of development plans provides an important opportunity to test the practicality and environmental acceptability of guideline figures at the local level.

**Planning for future after-uses**

10.8 In the past the allocation of land for mineral extraction has tended to be considered entirely separately from decisions on final after-use. Although after-uses should never be used as a justification for mineral working there is an opportunity for after-uses to contribute to wider plan objectives in a coordinated way. Mineral sites offer opportunities for habitat creation, landscape rehabilitation, and informal recreation. They also offer opportunities for taking pressure off more sensitive areas, for example making special provision for noisy sports or horse riding.

10.9 Coordinating after-uses with wider plan objectives depends to a large extent on widening the brief of those responsible for mineral planning to include a more detailed consideration of after-use earlier in the process. Planning the combination of after-uses may meet strategic objectives whereas considered individually there may be conflict between different after-uses and irrevocable erosion of the attractiveness of the area.

**Restoration and aftercare**

10.10 Regardless of location, development plan policies should seek to ensure that the very highest standards of

**Box 10.3 Example policy/justification on the after-use planning of mineral workings**

Chelmsford Borough Council included the following policy in its 1993 Local Plan Deposit Draft Written Statement:

RE9:
The Borough Council, in consultation with the Minerals Planning Authority, will identify preferred after-uses for mineral working sites in the Borough, in order to secure environmental enhancement and achieve high standards in the implementation of after-use schemes.

mineral restoration and aftercare are achieved in accordance with the provisions set out in the 1981 Town and Country Planning (Minerals) Act (as embodied in the Town and Country Planning Act, 1991) and in *The amenity reclamation of mineral workings*, DOE (1992).

10.11 With advanced reclamation techniques, it is now possible to minimise the impact of active mineral workings, to recreate many types of landscape and landscape features, and to create certain types of habitat. We are keen to ensure that these opportunities are maximised and that attention is focused on:

- promoting habitat creation, informal access, and the addition of landscape features characteristic of the area, as part of all reclamation schemes even when the primary emphasis may be on other after-uses

- designing restoration proposals to make a positive contribution and to fit well within their surroundings

10.12 It will also be important to ensure that an individual or organisation is available to take on long-term responsibility for any restored site and that sufficient funds are available to carry out the required management. Without this assurance there is no certainty that reclamation intentions will be carried through to reach maturity. Voluntary agreements (eg Section 106 agreements (Town and Country Planning Act 1990)) can play an important part in this, as in securing wider environmental gains. Useful information is included in the Countryside Commission's report *Opencast coal mining* (CCP 434 1993).

**Earth science interest**

10.13 A special feature of mineral workings can be their value for the earth sciences. Plans should indicate this potential and the need to respect this interest should it arise during working or subsequent restoration. Plans might indicate that planning conditions can be used to make a provision to allow submission of a revised working programme and restoration scheme if geological features of special significance are exposed. *Earth science conservation in Great Britain: a strategy* (including appendices) NCC (1991) offers advice

**Box 10.4 Example policy on restoration and aftercare**

Hampshire County Council included the following policy in the proposed pre-inquiry changes to the 1994 Minerals and Waste Local Plan, Deposit Plan:

16:
The County Council will normally grant planning permission for minerals and waste development in conformity with the other policies in the plan provided it is satisfied that where appropriate, adequate provision has been made for environmental enhancement and public benefits, particularly landscape improvements, enhancement, and creation of appropriate wildlife habitats, maintenance and enhancement of geological features, maintenance of important archaeological sites and monuments, improvement of existing and creation of new public access to land, and provision of land for local public amenity through:

- the restoration, aftercare and after-use of development sites
- the conservation and enhancement of the wider surrounding area to which the development site relates, and
- provision by the operator and/or landowner for the long-term maintenance and management of the land

The County Council will seek to ensure such enhancement and benefits by means of conditions attached to planning permissions or through planning obligations or other appropriate legal agreements.

## Waste disposal

10.14 For waste disposal, in the light of sustainability objectives we favour:

- emphasis on reducing the demand for waste disposal by waste recycling and reduction
- careful consideration of all environmental concerns in identifying waste disposal or waste treatment sites
- careful examination of the impacts of land-raising through land-fill
- positive use of landfill and reclamation schemes to achieve other environmental objectives

**Recycling**
10.15 *This common inheritance* set a Government target for recycling half of all household waste that can be recycled by the year 2000 (broadly 25% of all household waste). Local authorities are required to prepare a recycling plan for submission to the DOE by the Environmental Protection Act 1989 and there should be close liaison between Mineral Planning Authorities and Waste Regulation authorities regarding the recycling of mineral wastes (MPG 6 paragraph 38).

**Box 10.5 Local plan checklist for waste disposal**

If waste planning becomes a local authority function we would hope to see the following addressed in statutory plans:

- policies on waste reduction and recycling
- consideration of environmental capacity in waste planning
- the use of landfill to achieve wider environmental objectives
- policies on restoration and aftercare

10.16 We strongly support all moves towards waste reduction and recycling and believe that these principles should underpin all waste management strategies. The aim should be to reduce reliance on primary resources in production processes, save energy in waste transport, and reduce dependence on landfill as the main method of disposal. This means considering waste reduction and recycling at each stage in waste processing, with waste recovery occurring as close to its origin as possible so as to minimise transport requirements. Different approaches may need to be adopted in urban and rural areas.

**Environmental capacity in waste disposal planning**
10.17 Waste will continue to be disposed of by landfill and there is a need for thorough examination of the environmental impacts that will take place at different sites. Procedures similar to those that identify 'preferred areas' for minerals are appropriate. In particular:

- waste disposal should not generally occur in National Parks and AONBs except in exceptional circumstances where landfill is for local needs only and/or will help achieve desired restoration of past mineral workings

**Box 10.6 Example policy on recycling**

Bedfordshire County Council included the following policy in its 1994 Minerals and Waste Local Plan Deposit Draft (plus amendments):

MW38:
The County Council will positively encourage the recycling and reuse of waste. Suitable facilities will be provided at tidy tips and sought at other appropriate locations throughout the county.

- site selection for landfill should take full account of the earth science and biological interest of pits and quarries

- land-raising may be detrimental to archaeological interest and should be avoided in river floodplains where it results in unnatural landforms and may exacerbate flooding problems. In other areas its suitability should be judged against local landscape character.

10.18 An assessment of environmental capacity will need to reflect the policies for all aspects of environmental conservation and enhancement in the plan area. This will need to take account of both the direct effects of landfill and the potential indirect effects, such as changes to water table levels and pollution of groundwater. We believe local authorities should press for an Environmental Assessment to accompany all landfill proposals in or adjoining areas statutorily recognised for their conservation importance.

**Landfill and wider environmental objectives**

10.19 Use of waste disposal to achieve the reclamation of previously disturbed and possibly contaminated land can be of environmental benefit, both to solve pollution problems and to facilitate the positive use of sites which would otherwise remain under-utilised. Opportunities exist for creative after-use to benefit wildlife, landscape, and recreation. This suggests that waste planning should be developed alongside wider plan objectives to ensure that benefits are maximised.

10.20 In turn, as mineral working voids can sometimes offer a resource for waste disposal, there should be close liaison in the allocation of after-uses to new mineral sites and the planning of waste disposal. Mineral workings in environmentally sensitive locations should not normally have planned after-uses which require landfill. Conversely, new mineral workings close to urban areas and outside designated landscapes may be appropriate as landfill sites and after-use proposals should reflect this potential. Many derelict mineral workings and other forms of derelict land that might be used for waste disposal have acquired considerable nature conservation importance, both for biological and earth science interest. Many are SSSIs. These aspects should be fully taken into account when allocating land for waste disposal.

**Box 10.7 Example policy/justification on landfill and wider environmental objectives**

Dartford Borough Council included the following policy in its 1991 Local Plan Deposit Written Statement:

WD1:
The Council will seek to ensure that any proposals for waste disposal take full account of their local impact, especially on the environment, amenity, nature conservation, and road network. There is a presumption against proposals for disposal by landfill of non-inert waste. Any such proposals which may be exceptionally justified must establish:

- a need for a disposal facility

- that landfill is appropriate and acceptable for the particular site concerned

- that alternatives to landfill, including incineration and recycling, have been investigated, evaluated, and proved to be non-viable

- compliance with the NRA's requirements in relation to the protection of water supply boreholes

Any proposals should deal comprehensively with landfill gas generation and incorporate restoration landscaping and aftercare proposals. In any landfill proposal, the Council will look for appropriate financial or other legally binding guarantees from operators that the necessary restoration and landscaping work will be carried out.

**Restoration and aftercare**

10.21 The highest standards of restoration and aftercare should be sought for landfill sites. If there is serious doubt whether satisfactory reclamation can be achieved at a particular site, then permission for landfill should not be granted. Restoration and aftercare proposals should respect existing features and habitats of conservation interest on the site and their retention might well form part of planning conditions. In general, similar considerations apply as for minerals aftercare.

# Chapter 11 Tourism and active recreation or sport

## Introduction

11.1 This chapter deals with aspects of tourism and recreation which involve development or change of land use. Informal recreation involving access to and enjoyment of the countryside has close links with policies on conservation and is therefore considered separately in Chapter 5.

11.2 England's landscape, natural and cultural heritage, and built environment are part of the nation's soul: they are also our greatest tourism assets, and there is a clear and positive relationship between tourism and maintaining and enhancing the environment. Tourism can provide a strong impetus for environmental enhancement, including the restoration of historic buildings, the conservation of past industrial areas, and the cleaning up of rivers. It also provides economic support for local people and in so doing can reinforce local culture and local distinctiveness. On the other hand, if insensitively handled, it can lead to a rapid dilution of local character, cause grave damage to sensitive areas, and threaten the very qualities which drew visitors in the first place. Likewise, many sports offer a way of enjoying rural surroundings and many of the more attractive parts of the countryside provide important resources for active recreation. There are limits, however, to the capacity of some areas to accommodate such activities without detriment to their character and quality or to the enjoyment of others.

## Tourism

11.3 Many aspects of tourism may be best covered in a non-statutory strategy. Local plans, however, will need to cover the land use implications of tourism as set out in PPG 21, *Tourism*. It is not our role to make comments on levels of provision but the implications for the environment must be fully addressed in local plans.

**Box 11.1 Local plan checklist for tourism**

We would expect local plans to contain policies on the following topics, in all cases reflecting their interface with conservation interests:

- tourism which invests in the natural and cultural heritage of an area (promotion of green or sustainable tourism)
- managing tourism in historic towns
- major new built tourism attractions
- visitor accommodation
- farm tourism
- outdoor education and pursuit centres, where appropriate
- camping and caravanning

11.4 The general principles which we would hope to see influencing tourism planning are:

- guiding different types of tourism development to suitable locations
- identifying environmental capacity for tourism of different parts of plan areas
- retaining undisturbed wild and remote areas valued by visitors
- ensuring that all tourism development respects the character of the locality without damaging landscape, nature conservation or archaeological, historical or cultural interests
- being aware of the cumulative effect on the landscape of many otherwise small tourist developments
- encouraging tourism that draws on and reinforces the character of town and country and promotes understanding of the environment
- diverting pressures on 'honeypot' locations by promoting a more even spread of tourist attractions
- reducing reliance on the private car by locating major attractions, as far as possible, close to public transport links and promoting public transport as the best method of getting around
- encouraging longer stay and off-peak visits which can contribute most to the maintenance of a healthy local economy and built environment
- identifying positive opportunities for management to avoid or reduce conflict between tourism and conservation

11.5 Nearly all aspects of a local plan will have a direct bearing on tourism, from policies relating to conservation of the natural and built environment (Chapter 3 and 4) to policies covering transport (Chapter 6) and the countryside (Chapter 8). There will therefore need to be consistency between tourism and the other policy objectives of the plan.

**Investing in the natural and cultural heritage of an area (green or sustainable tourism)**
11.6 We believe that the principles of green or sustainable tourism should lie at the heart of all local

**Box 11.2 Example policy on tourism and the natural and cultural heritage of an area**

East Lindsey District Council included the following policy in its 1994 Local Plan Deposit Copy (plus proposed amendments):

T1:
Development proposals for leisure and tourism uses will normally be permitted where they:

- consolidate and expand coastal holiday tourism and visitor facilities centred on Mablethorpe and Skegness
- reinforce existing visitor facilities, at a locally appropriate scale, at Woodhall Spa, Tattershall, North Somercotes, Saltfleet, Anderby Creek, Sutton-on-Sea, Trusthorpe, Chapel St Leonards, and Ingoldmells
- promote the heritage of the historic market towns of Louth, Alford, Horncastle, and Spilsby
- provide for visitor quiet enjoyment of the countryside
- while, at the same time and in every case, they have due regard to protecting the district's natural and heritage assets and the amenities of local communities.

planning. Green or sustainable tourism is defined by the Countryside Commission as:

- socially and environmentally considerate
- drawing on the natural beauty and character of the area
- small in scale and developing slowly
- supporting the local economy and employing local people
- caring about quality
- bringing conservation and recreation benefits
- reusing existing buildings and derelict land
- favouring public transport
- and, importantly, developing at a pace and scale which ensures that the assets of the area (both natural and cultural) are not diminished in the long term

11.7 Although this definition primarily relates to rural areas this approach has equal relevance to those urban areas of architectural and historic importance which are of particular concern to us. The relationship between tourism and conservation issues is reviewed in, among other sources, *Tourism and the environment - maintaining the balance*, English Tourist Board and Employment Department Group (1991), *The Green Light - a guide to sustainable tourism*, English Tourist Board, Countryside Commission, Rural Development Commission, and *Tourism in National Parks: a guide to good practice*, Countryside Commission, Countryside Council for Wales, English Tourist Board, Wales Tourist Board, and the Rural Development Commission (1991).

**Managing tourism in historic towns**

11.8 Historic towns and cities are one of our key tourism assets, attracting many millions of visitors a year. None the less, this tourism has major implications for the character and durability of historic towns. Studies of tourism in cities such as Chester have indicated the types of problem which need to be addressed, including wear and tear, pedestrian congestion, parking problems, inappropriate uses for old buildings, and the influence of shop fronts. Such problems can adversely effect visitor enjoyment and have longer-term implications for the built fabric.

11.9 When relevant, local plans should include policies to address these pressures, potentially indicating that separate tourism strategies will be developed for historic town centres. Policies for managing tourism in historic towns will need to be closely linked with those concerned with conserving the built fabric (Chapter 3 and 4) and with transport, especially policies associated with road closures, pedestrianisation and pedestrian priority, park and ride, and parking.

**New tourism attractions**

11.10 Although we support green tourism, we recognise that there will continue to be a market for mass tourism, from holiday villages to theme parks. Development to meet this demand usually relies on proximity to large markets and good infrastructure. It is unrelated to the inherent qualities of an area, and is therefore best located within or on the edge of urban areas, away from areas of environmental sensitivity.

**Box 11.3 Example policy on managing tourism in historic towns**

Oxford City Council included the following policy in its 1993 Deposit Local Plan Review 1991-2001:

TO3:
The Council will encourage tourists to use park and ride services, in particular by using planning powers:

- providing sites for travel, parking, and tourist information at park and ride car parks
- seeking clearer road signing to park and ride
- encouraging the provision of visitor accommodation in the vicinity of park and ride car parks where compatible with other planning polices

**Box 11.4 Example policy on new tourism attractions**

Hambleton District Council included the following policy in its 1994 Deposit Draft District Wide Local Plan:

TO6:
Large-scale tourist attractions such as theme parks and residential holiday centres will not normally be permitted. Exceptionally, where there are significant proven benefits to the local economy and employment which other policies of the plan would be unlikely to achieve, proposals will be permitted provided that all of the following criteria are met:

- they are not within the AONBs, Special Landscape Areas, parks and gardens of historic or landscape interest, or the Green Belt
- they relate sympathetically to the scale and level of activity in the locality
- they will not adversely affect the character or appearance of the countryside
- they will not result in a detrimental impact on road safety and the free flow of traffic on the highway network or require improvement which could detrimentally affect the character of rural roads in the area generally
- they will not have an adverse impact on the character or setting of settlements or the amenity of existing residents
- they will not have an adverse impact on sites of nature conservation value or archaeological importance or buildings of architectural or historic interest
- any new buildings are of a good standard of design and are sympathetic to the landscape in terms of their design, siting, and materials
- they do not result in the loss of the best and most versatile agricultural land

In all cases a full environmental assessment of the proposal will be required.

11.11 Such developments should be guided away from designated areas including National Parks and AONBs, which in recent years have been under increasing pressure from large self-sufficient holiday complexes and the like. On the other hand they can provide the impetus for the reclamation of derelict land in suitable locations provided that this approach is not allowed to encourage dereliction as a means of securing permission to develop land. The potential interest of derelict land for nature conservation including the earth sciences should be taken into account. The industrial archaeological interest of some derelict land may be a positive tourism asset. It is not only the impact of the development itself which is of concern but the ripple effect of improved road junctions to localised road widening, all of which have a suburbanising influence resulting in dilution of local character.

**Box 11.5 Example policy on tourism accommodation**

The North York Moors National Park Authority included the following policy in its 1992 Local Plan:

TR1:
Proposals for new tourist accommodation (or the extension of existing establishments) will only be permitted within the National Park where the development:

- is of a scale appropriate to the existing level of activity in the area
- is of a type and design which will not adversely affect the landscape and built environment of the locality
- does not conflict with other policies of the local plan

New development in open countryside or any large-scale development will not be considered acceptable in principle within the National Park.

**Visitor accommodation**

11.12 As for all other forms of development, we do not believe that tourism provides a justification for new buildings in the open countryside. Tourist accommodation should be provided on land allocated for development within existing settlements or through the conversion of appropriate buildings. New time-share developments and holiday villages should be strongly resisted in the open countryside, except in exceptional circumstances.

**Farm tourism**

11.13 Farms are playing an increasingly important role in tourism. Farm tourism provides a means of supporting the farm and the wider rural economy and promoting the inherent attractions of an area. For some farms, especially those in marginal farming areas, income from tourism can exceed that from agriculture and is essential for maintaining farm viability. Farm tourism is to be welcomed where it does not compromise the environment through, for example, a proliferation of new farm buildings under permitted development rights, or the inappropriate conversion of buildings of historic or architectural importance. Some of these issues are discussed in Chapter 8.

### Outdoor education and pursuit centres

11.14 Outdoor education and pursuit centres have traditionally been located in National Parks and other areas of high scenic quality. Such centres are important in helping people, especially the young and disadvantaged, to visit, learn about, and enjoy the rural environment. Unfortunately, such centres may sometimes inadvertently lead to damage of sensitive environments through disturbance or excessive use. Any new centres should therefore be located in areas where the environment has the capacity to absorb these activities. Consideration should also be given to encouraging their location close to main centres of population, thus making them more accessible on a regular basis and reducing travel needs.

### Camping and caravan sites

11.15 Static caravan and chalet sites can be highly intrusive. We believe, therefore, that the development of new facilities of this nature should be resisted, especially in designated areas, along the open coastline and within the setting of buildings or designed landscapes of historic importance. Emphasis should be placed instead on trying to improve the environmental acceptability of existing sites. This might be achieved by a general policy on relocation of existing intrusive sites and by attaching appropriate conditions to permissions to improve, extend or upgrade their facilities. The objective should be to secure:

- relocation of pitches away from the most visible parts of the site
- improved standards of landscaping and site treatment appropriate to the location, which may require an increased site area, by allowing the present number of pitches to remain but at a lower density

11.16 Touring caravan sites tend not to be so intrusive in the landscape as static sites, being generally of a smaller scale, with caravans removed during the winter and problems of off-season storage being largely avoided. Nevertheless, the provision of new touring caravan and camping sites should be judged against strict criteria and further provision avoided in areas which are already well provided for and/or in landscapes considered by the local authority to be particularly sensitive to this form of development.

11.17 The environmental criteria against which new touring caravan and camping sites might be judged include:

- avoidance of sensitive landscapes and areas with already adequate provision
- an appropriate site in landscape terms
- well related to the existing road network
- not necessitating insensitive highway improvements
- only used for an eight-month period (March to October) with all standings and caravans removed outside this period
- as far as possible, relying on the conversion of existing traditional buildings to provide the required facilities

## Active recreation and sport

11.18 Advice on active recreation and sport is primarily the responsibility of the Sports Council and the planning requirements of sport are set out in PPG 17, *Sport and recreation*. Our aim is not to repeat this PPG but to look at the relationship between sport and the environment.

11.19 Increasing use is made of the countryside for active recreation and sport. These activities cover an enormous range, from those which require little in the way of fixed facilities, such as ballooning and rock climbing, to those which require specific facilities and cover substantial areas of land, such as golf courses

**Box 11.6 Example policy on camping and caravan sites**

East Lindsey District Council included the following policy in its 1994 proposed amendments to the Deposit Local Plan:

T16:
Outside the areas defined in policies T2 and T14, the use of land for touring caravans or camping will normally be permitted provided that:

- it is within an area defined as a touring caravans site on a proposals inset map
- it is associated with an existing residential use
- it is associated with an existing visitor attraction but does not dominate because of its siting, scale or location
- it is located in or alongside the settlements identified in Policy T1(b) and in every case:
    - it has easy access to the strategic road network and avoids the use of narrow country lanes
    - it does not harm the amenities of any adjacent dwellings because of its siting, scale, noise or traffic generation
    - it is accompanied by an informal landscaping scheme which shows how the impact of the development is reduced on the wider landscape
    - any associated built development is incorporated into or forms an extension to an existing building

**Box 11.7 Local plan checklist for active recreation and sport**

Our concern is to ensure that plans contain policies relating to those active recreational activities which most directly impinge on our areas of interest, namely, and where appropriate:

- golf courses and related developments
- marina developments
- potentially disruptive sports
- commercial riding establishments

and artificial ski slopes. Our concern is to ensure that such activities can be accommodated without detriment to the character and quality of the area or to the quiet enjoyment of others. In particular we are keen to:

- ensure that sports facilities (such as golf courses) which cover substantial areas of land and which can lead to a change in landscape character, potential loss of habitats, and the addition of ancillary development are located with greatest care
- minimise the development of major built facilities for sport in the open countryside and ensure that ancillary buildings for outdoor activities remain ancillary and are of an appropriate scale
- avoid damage to sensitive sites by roving activities which frequently operate under the 28-or 14-day rule, for example war games, orienteering, off-road motor sports, etc

11.20 In seeking the most suitable location for different sporting activities we hope that in the preparation of local plans consideration is given to:

- ensuring that the environmental capacity of different areas to accept sporting and recreation facilities is assessed, with facilities being guided to where they will cause least environmental damage
- ensuring that the level of demand actually justifies the provision of sports facilities
- ensuring that there is liaison with surrounding local authorities where facilities are serving more than a local catchment, to allow the choice of the most suitable site to extend across local authority boundaries, so as to minimise impact on the environment and maximise opportunities for connecting to the public transport network

11.21 We are also keen to maximise the added value of recreation and sporting provision by:

- wherever possible combining provision for sport with that for nature conservation and/or increased access, including the multiple use of buildings for sport and environmental education and the multiple use of land and water through time and space zoning
- ensuring that environmental conservation and enhancement measures are incorporated as part of the design of new sports and recreation facilities

**Golf courses and golf driving ranges**

11.22 Golf courses require substantial areas of land (eg 50-60 ha for an 18-hole course) and inevitably involve changes in landscape character associated with the remodelling of local topography and the introduction of artificial features and special maintenance regimes. Valuable wildlife habitats, historical and archaeological features, and geological and physiographic features can be damaged or destroyed, either directly or indirectly, for example by drainage works, and golf course irrigation can make substantial demands on local water supplies. Registered historic parks and gardens, often associated with a listed mansion house, have been especially vulnerable to damage from this type of development.

11.23 For these reasons we believe new golf course developments should not be considered in National Parks, AONBs, the Broads, the New Forest, and Heritage Coasts, except where it can be demonstrated that the proposal would positively contribute to and enhance the special character of the area. They should be opposed where they threaten the integrity of historic landscapes and archaeological complexes or the viability of important habitats. Where golf courses directly affect nationally designated landscapes we believe they should be the subject of an environmental assessment. Some habitats and landscape types can absorb golf courses without significant impact, and in degraded environments golf courses may offer a positive opportunity for environmental enhancement. Golf courses may also provide an important buffer between housing and agricultural land and between housing and areas of nature or archaeological importance, and on occasion may be preferable on archaeological grounds to continued arable use.

11.24 Large-scale built development, including luxury housing, hotels, conference centres, and sports facilities, is often proposed in association with golf courses in locations where they would otherwise be refused, sometimes on the grounds that these facilities are required to maintain the viability of the course. Such built development should be strongly resisted in the open countryside and any arguments relating to its importance to viability should be very carefully scrutinised.

11.25 All golf course developments should be judged against strict environmental criteria. These criteria should:

- provide for a sufficiently large site to avoid over-development and to allow proper management of roughs and general landscaping

- be designed to conserve existing landscape and historical features and habitats of value

**Box 11.8 Example policy on golf course development**

Hambleton District Council included the following policy in its 1994 Deposit Draft District Wide Local Plan:

SR6:
New golf courses or driving ranges and extensions to existing courses will be permitted provided that the proposal meets all of the following criteria:

- it is designed and located to ensure harmony and good visual integration with the surrounding countryside and it will not adversely affect the character and appearance of the countryside

- it makes provision for the retention and management of important landscape features and any landscaping reflects the area's character in form and choice of species

- it will not result in the loss of the best and most versatile agricultural land

- it will not adversely affect sites of nature conservation value or archaeological or historic importance

- any new buildings and hardstandings are essential to the functioning of the golf course and are of a high standard of design

- it will not result in a volume of traffic which exceeds the capacity of the surrounding road network or requires changes to the road network which will adversely affect the character of the area

- it will not adversely affect the amenity of residents in the vicinity

- it will not adversely affect the enjoyment of other users of the countryside, particularly those using the public rights-of-way network.

Proposals in the AONBs, Special Landscape Areas, parks and gardens of historic or landscape interest, SSSIs, and the Green Belt will not be permitted when they are incompatible with the objectives behind these designations.

Applicants must demonstrate that the proposal is viable in its own right and will not require additional development to support it.

- be designed to avoid adverse impacts on existing public access

- be designed to reflect local landscape character

- include specific proposals for environmental enhancement such as new habitat features and additional footpath links

11.26 We would also like to see separate policies developed on golf driving ranges. Although covering very much smaller areas, they can have considerable impact, sometimes involving large buildings, high perimeter fencing, and floodlighting, and are usually not suited to locations in the open countryside. All three agencies have produced useful publications on golf courses: *On course conservation: managing golf's natural heritage*, NCC (1990), *Golf courses in the countryside*, Countryside Commission (CCP 438, 1993), *Golf course proposals in historic landscapes*, English Heritage (undated).

**Marina developments**
11.27 Reference has already been made to our concern for the conservation of rivers, estuaries, and the undeveloped coastline, especially sites of national and international importance for landscape and/or wildlife and the riverine and marine/intertidal archaeological resource. There is a continuing demand for new marina provision but this should be limited to areas which do not conflict with conservation interests, for example by locating them within existing harbours, through the conversion of redundant commercial and naval dockyards where this does not compromise historic interest, and through the creation of new pools on adjacent redundant farmland. We are also keen to see a distinction made between housing developments with associated marina facilities, which usually have little to do with meeting the demands of the sport and may actually displace boats to other locations, and those proposals aimed specifically at meeting the minimum requirements of the genuine sailor.

11.28 In the future, the suitability of development in individual estuaries should be guided by an estuary

**Box 11.9 Example policy on marina development**

The 1992 Poole Coastal Local Plan included the following policy:

10.22:
The Borough Council will consider proposals to extend existing marina, jetty, slipway or other boating and mooring facilities on their merits, having regard to the impact of the development on the interests of the other harbour users, on the ecological value of the harbour and on views across the harbour currently available to residents and visitors.

management plan, with the lead normally being taken by local authorities and aimed at securing the sustainable management of the estuary under consideration. We would also expect all major marina developments to be the subject of an environmental assessment.

Useful references on estuary management plans from English Nature are *A strategy for the sustainable use of England's estuaries* (1993), *Estuary management plans - a co-ordinator's guide* (1993), *Conserving England's marine heritage - a strategy* (1993).

**Potentially disruptive sports**

11.29 There are a number of sporting activities which, because of noise generation, erosion, and/or general disturbance, can be particularly disruptive to nature conservation and the enjoyment of the countryside and may lead to erosion of archaeological sites. These include off-road motor sports (two-wheel and four-wheel), target and clay pigeon shooting, paint-ball (or war) games, and certain water sports including jet-skiing and power boats.

11.30 The majority of the land-based activities named above take place under the 28- or 14-day rule for the temporary use of land, in accordance with the General Development Order 1988, and therefore lie outside planning control. The management and location of such facilities should nevertheless be given careful consideration in relevant non-statutory strategies, in association with the governing bodies of these sports. Where such activities are causing major disruption to conservation interests and/or the enjoyment of the countryside or where there is clear local demand, consideration should be given to providing a permanent year-round facility to take pressure off more sensitive areas. Such facilities should be located close to the population which they are serving, in robust environments where the noise can be contained, for example old quarry sites, or where there are already high ambient noise levels, for example close to main roads. Possible sites could be identified in local plans. Where serious environmental damage is being caused by these activities, the written justification of the local plan could indicate the willingness of the local authority to use Article 4 directions to try and control these activities.

11.31 By comparison with land-based activities, noisy sports on inland waters are normally permanent, with fixed facilities, and they are therefore subject to planning control. The suitability of such activities should be given careful consideration. In our view they are generally inappropriate in designated landscapes or close to areas of high nature conservation importance and strong emphasis should be placed on noise attenuation measures. Planning conditions or planning obligations should be used to ensure that noise levels remain within defined limits through noise attenuation measures, specifying times of operation, and setting maximum acceptable noise levels as agreed in consultation with the governing body for that sport.

**Box 11.10 Example policy on potentially disruptive sports**

East Lindsey District Council included the following policy in its 1994 proposed amendments to the Deposit Local Plan:

REC11:
The development of noisy sport or recreation uses, particularly involving the use of motorised vehicles or firearms, will not be permitted within the Coastal Conservation Areas, the Wolds AONB, or within or adjacent to nature reserves or other important sites of wildlife habitat or nature interest, unless where, in exceptional circumstances:

- it is essential to be in that location and cannot be located elsewhere
- it can be developed so that the character, appearance and quiet enjoyment of the locality remains unharmed
- the nature conservation importance of the site would remain essentially unaffected

Elsewhere, such a use will normally be permitted provided:

- it is adjacent to existing higher than normal noise generating uses and does not raise the ambient noise levels
- it is located where the existing topography or landscape forms an effective noise barrier
- noise attenuation measures are incorporated to reduce ambient noise levels to an acceptable level
- it does not harm the residential amenities of the area

In all cases, conditions will be attached to any planning permission, or a planning obligation entered into, to ensure that no successive alteration to the development will cause a noise problem.

**Commercial riding establishments**

11.32 Horse riding offers an attractive way of exploring the countryside, but attendant problems may arise in the case of commercial riding establishments and livery yards. These can be quite substantial developments with stabling, flood-lit exercise areas, and indoor riding schools, and even demands for new housing to allow a 24-hour presence on site. In some cases, however, commercial establishments can be a positive force in maintaining traditional pastoral landscapes, especially where there is a commitment to good pasture management and fence maintenance. For these reasons we believe that the suitability of new commercial horse riding establishments should be judged against local circumstances.

11.33 The specific criteria against which new commercial horse riding establishments should be judged include:

- an appropriate scale and design in keeping with the locality
- sited to take advantage of existing screening and well integrated with existing buildings
- based on a compact building layout
- located in an area with sufficient suitable routes or land for riding in the vicinity without exacerbating pressure on already overused areas
- incorporating sufficient grazing land as part of the overall development to allow for good pasture management and rotational grazing

**Box 11.11 Example policy on commercial riding establishments**

East Lindsey District Council included the following policy in its 1994 proposed amendments to the Deposit Local Plan:

REC14:
Development of commercial horse riding facilities will normally be permitted where:

- a minimum of 1.5 acres (0.6 hectares) of grazing land per horse or pony is available
- it uses existing buildings or where new buildings are proposed they are sited next to existing buildings or otherwise visually form an integral part of the overall development
- it is accompanied by an integrated landscaping scheme and boundary treatment will incorporate Lincolnshire post and rail fencing, deciduous hedge or brick walling
- accessible and adequate off-road trails are available in the form of bridleways or private agreements
- it does not materially harm the amenities of the nearby area by reason of noise, smell, traffic generation or visual intrusion